I Love You, Miss Huddleston

And Other Inappropriate Longings of My Indiana Childhood

Philip Gulley

HarperOne
An Imprint of HarperCollins*Publishers*

Names and identifying details of the individuals discussed in this book have been changed to protect their privacy.

HarperCollins books may be purchased for educational, business, or sales promotional use. For information, please e-mail the Special Markets Department at SPsales@harpercollins.com.

HarperCollins Web site: http://www.harpercollins.com

Interior Design: Laura Lind Design

FIRST HARPERCOLLINS PAPERBACK EDITION PUBLISHED IN 2010

Library of Congress Cataloging-in-Publication Data
Gulley, Philip.
I love you, Miss Huddleston, and other inappropriate longings of my Indiana childhood / Philip Gulley. — 1st ed.
p. cm.

1. Gulley, Philip—Childhood and youth. 2. Gulley, Philip—Homes and haunts—Indiana. 3. Authors, American—20th century—Biography. 4. Danville (Ind.)—Biography. 5. Danville (Ind.)—Social life and customs. I. Title.
PS3557.U449Z46 2009
813'.54—dc22
[B]

ISBN: 978-0-06-180955-2

16 17 18 19 RRD(H) 10 9 8 7 6 5 4

Contents

Preface

In his book, *Too Soon Old, Too Late Smart,* Gordon Livingston writes, "Memory is not, as many of us think, an accurate transcription of past experience. Rather it is a story we tell ourselves about the past, full of distortions, wishful thinking, and unfulfilled dreams." *I Love You, Miss Huddleston* is the story I have told myself about my adolescence.

Those who shared those years with me might remember them differently. That is their prerogative, just as it is my right to make things more lively than they might have been. I am probably a little more exciting in the following pages than I was in real life.

This is not a careful narrative, meticulously following the march of days. Nor is this history. It is story, and story has a way of shifting with the sands of time. I've never kept a diary, just a few scribbled notes in the dusty archives of my mind. Some things I report happening at the age of twelve might well have taken place when I was fourteen. For the sake of fun, I've exaggerated some of my exploits. It will be obvious to the reader when I've strayed from the path of truth.

Regarding names: I've changed some and kept others. When I felt the use of a real name might cause embarrassment, I changed it. I altered a few descriptions for the same reason.

What I didn't change was the sense of freedom I felt as a child. I don't know what today's children will remember. I suspect their recollections will consist mostly of one carefully scripted day after another, of tediously regimented weeks, of dampened opportunities for spontaneity and unbridled fun. I sometimes wonder if my generation was the last one to live freely, before the "child industry" seduced parents into spending vast amounts of money to ensure their child's emotional well-being. The timing of my birth couldn't have been better—with no one guiding my every step, my childhood was one of unrelieved and happy chaos.

It's been said that a miserable life makes for good writing. If that is so, my parents failed to groom me for this vocation. They did, however, prepare me for deep satisfaction. For that, and for much more, I dedicate this book to them, Norman and Gloria Gulley, in hopes they'll forgive me for exaggerating their peculiarities in order to earn my living.

I dedicate this book also to the memory of Jim Land, educator and friend, who left this world too soon.

Chapter 1

My Perilous Start

When I was four months old, a few days after a photographer had taken my baby picture, my father lost his job. When the photographer returned bearing the proofs for my parents to choose from, they could no longer afford the photos. The man took pity and gave them a proof for free, which my parents displayed on our living room wall, alongside pictures of my siblings. I wore a cute little Onesie. My right hand was extended in a posture of blessing, a beatific smile lay upon my features, purple ink etched the word *PROOF* across my belly. Adding to this indignity, I was afflicted with cradle cap, which, in combination with a stray shadow, gave me the appearance of wearing a yarmulke. I looked like a miniature rabbi whom the Lord, in that fickle way of the Divine, had placed among the Gentiles. Like my brothers and sister, I was baptized Catholic, though I now believe that was done to throw me off.

When I was old enough to notice my picture, I asked why I was branded so peculiarly.

Glenn, my oldest brother, took it upon himself to explain this and other mysteries to me. "You're not one of us," he said. "Someone left you in a banana box on our front porch."

"We thought someone had given us bananas," my father said. "It was a real disappointment."

Shaken by this revelation, I looked at my mother.

"We love you just the same," she said, patting me on the head.

Thus, I was as Moses among the Egyptians, set adrift in the reeds, a stranger in a strange land.

As a young child I was prone to illness, lurching from one infirmity to another. After one was healed, another rose and took its place. When I was finally healed of the cradle cap, my eyes became inexplicably crossed and my legs turned inward. My mother drove me to Indianapolis to the Shimp Optical Company, where I was fitted with binocular-like glasses. A few weeks later, splints were lashed to my legs and I lay on my back for several days, like a bug-eyed beetle stunned by a spritz of Raid, which is where I was when John F. Kennedy was shot. But I had my own problems and gave his predicament little thought.

In addition to my poor vision and limited mobility, I had

a profound speech impediment and could barely make myself understood. My parents employed a speech therapist who came to our home each Thursday and had me repeat words with the letter *r.*

"The wed caw dwove down the gwavel woad," I would say, over and over again.

The therapist, a Mr. Wobewt Fowtnew, eventually diagnosed me with a weak tongue that couldn't curl sufficiently to make the *r* sound. He advised my mother to have me take up bubble gum and brought a bag of Bazooka each week for me to chew. This gave me little incentive to correct the problem, and I continued to suffer.

Suffering was the common theme of that decade—the 1960s. Although my parents tried to hide its more violent aspects from us, I sensed something nefarious was under way. It had been our custom to watch Walter Cronkite after supper, but more and more often my siblings and I were shooed outside to play, where we would consult with the other children about world affairs.

Tom Keen—who lived three doors down, was four years older than I, and knew everything there was to know—told us we were at war, fighting the communists in Vietnam. I wasn't sure who the communists were, but knew they were bad since we had drills at school in the event they attacked us. Ours was a passive resistance—we crouched in the hallway, hands over our heads, until the theoretical bombs stopped falling and Mr. Michaels, our principal, came on the intercom to tell us it was safe to return to our desks.

Mr. Vaughn, our immediate neighbor, blamed every social ill on the commies. I deduced from him that communists had long hair, didn't bathe, listened to rock music, and lived, not only in Vietnam, but also in California, which I looked up in the atlas my father kept next to his recliner. California seemed perilously close, less than a foot from Indiana. I would lie awake at night, worrying about the communists and their near proximity.

The communists weren't the only threat to our well-being. Mr. Vaughn also warned us about the Japanese. "Gotta watch those little Nippers. Turn our backs on 'em for a second and they'll sneak attack us. Feisty little devils, the whole lot of 'em." Mr. Vaughn had a German shepherd named King, ostensibly to protect him against the Japanese and communists. But I fed him dog biscuits through the fence and we were thicker than thieves, King and I.

Despite these threats to my well-being, I reached the age of seven and went with my father to the town dump on a Saturday morning in search of a bicycle. Doc Foster, our town's garbage man, guided us past heaps of trash, scavenging various parts of bicycles until we had enough components to fashion suitable transportation. It was, when we finished assembling it, an object of kaleidoscope beauty—a Schwinn Typhoon, consisting of a green, slightly bent frame, two tires of differing sizes, a blue back fender and a yellow front one, and Sting-Ray handlebars. The bike lacked a seat, adding to its uniqueness, so I learned to ride standing up.

Thus equipped, I set out with my brothers to explore

our surroundings, riding east down Mill Street and north on Jefferson to the Danner's Five and Dime, where we visited the parrots and listened while hoodlums taught them dirty words. The hoodlums not only led the birds astray, they played pinball, an activity I have ever since associated with moral delinquency.

Across Main Street from Danner's was Lemmie Chalfant's plumbing shop, where Lemmie's wife, Violet, planted geraniums in a toilet bowl on the sidewalk outside their front door. Three doors south of the plumbing shop was the Buckhorn Bar. We would pause from our travel and peer into the smoky recesses of the tavern, watching the ghostly figures move about, the silence punctuated by an occasional burst of wild, intoxicated laughter. We were captivated by the depravity—swearing parrots, the swirl of tavern smoke, the yeasty scent of beer spilling through the door of the Buckhorn onto the town square—and would stand at the door until the bartender, Raymond Page, yelled at us to leave.

Kitty-corner from the Buckhorn was the Abstract and Title Building, in whose basement Floyd Jennings sold bicycles to the rich kids, the very bikes we peasants would eventually cannibalize, living off the dregs of other people's prosperity. The rich kids lived on Broadway Street, which the old timers called Millionaires' Row. When the town was platted, it had been named South Street, but when the moneyed class settled there, they desired a more illustrious address and the name was changed to Broadway.

It was nine blocks long, on the south side of town,

running parallel to Main Street. Smack in the center of Broadway sat the county jail, where Sheriff Merle Funk and his family lived in the front rooms and the prisoners resided in the rear. On the street side of the jail was a dog kennel, where the police dog lived. The dog had misplaced loyalties and would hurl himself at the fence in a mad effort to rip out the throats of elderly women strolling past, while being positively friendly to the inmates. The inmates appreciated his devotion and, not wanting to hurt the dog's feelings, never tried escaping.

My brothers and I would pedal our bicycles by the jail, stopping to aggravate the dog before entering the prosperous end of Broadway, riding through a tunnel of oak and maple trees, past movie-star homes with large porches set back from the street. It was clear we were trespassers, that we didn't belong there with our cobbled-together bicycles. I imagined what it might be like living in one of those houses, like Richie Rich, who I'd read about at the Danner's Five and Dime, even though Tom Keen had told me that reading a comic book without paying for it was against the law, the same as stealing.

One summer afternoon, while riding down Broadway, I stopped to rest. The disadvantage of riding a bicycle with no seat was that periodic breaks were required to restore one's vigor. A lady exited a home and walked down her sidewalk, greeting me as she approached. To my surprise, she knew my name, though she didn't say how. She was very kind and lovely, in a refined sort of way. I never told anyone about her, but suspected she was my real mother, who'd been caught up in a torrid affair of which I was the product, and to avoid scandal she'd left me in a banana box on the doorstep of a poor family, where I would not be materially blessed, but would be loved, for the most part.

For the next few years, I expected her to reclaim me, to rescue me from the Papists, and take me to my true home, where I would be given my rightful due—a new, one-color bicycle with its very own seat, all the Richie Rich comic books I could read, and various other treasures beyond my current reach. But apparently my real mother loved me too much to uproot me, so I was raised among the Gentiles and learned their ways, though always in the back of my mind was the conviction that my true home was on Broadway Street, among the well-to-do.

Chapter 2

Our New Digs

In the winter of 1970, when I was nine years old, our family moved across town to Broadway Street. Like every momentous event of my youth, a myth soon developed around that occurrence, and for a number of years I was led to believe my father had won the house in a poker game. Dad had a flair for enriching the most mundane events with bald exaggerations, all of which I believed. The poker story made a certain sense to me—the change in our circumstances was so magical it defied any logical explanation. It was the stuff of fairy tales, as if a prince had knocked on our door and placed the glass slipper on our foot for a perfect fit.

In later years, I would accompany my father on his Saturday morning visits to the First National Bank, where, Margery Poer, the teller, would give me a root beer sucker, then transact business with my father while I watched. When I grew old enough to know what the word *mortgage* meant, I knew we had gotten our house the same way everyone else had gotten theirs, through hard work and monthly payments. But my dad was a storyteller, and winning it in a poker game seemed so much more exotic. That was the history I preferred.

Before we moved into the house, we went to view it. The key to the front door was a skeleton key that had been lost shortly after the house was built in 1913. The previous owners had moved and taken the back door key with them, leaving the house open to whomever wanted to poke around. This open-door policy continued for as long as my parents lived there. They've returned home to find a woman afflicted with Alzheimer's drinking coffee in their kitchen, a peeping Tom in a closet, shirt-tail relatives, neighborhood children, and a snake. Each intrusion was handled with an unruffled poise—the Alzheimer's lady was returned to the nursing home, the peeping Tom sent packing, the relatives and neighborhood children fed, the snake cornered and set loose behind the barn. So on our first visit we did what everyone else felt free to do—walked right in and went to snooping.

My initial impression of our new home was one of vastness. Everything about the house was writ large—the front parlors, the staircase, the two fireplaces, the porch, the attic, the towering trees on the three-acre lawn, the barn—great yawning expanses of house and yard. It seemed, to my nine-year-old sensibilities, as if we had purchased a castle.

While we children explored the house, my parents walked from room to room flipping on a light switch here, turning on a faucet there. "Looks fine to me," my father announced after a few moments.

"What about those water stains?" asked my mother, peering at the kitchen ceiling. For the next thirty-four years, the stains would appear, disappear, then reappear mysteriously at the worst possible time, usually before a dinner party.

My father stared at the ceiling. "That's nothing, Glo. A little paint will cover that right up."

Paint was Dad's answer to every household repair. Layer upon layer, applied to leaking pipes, dented plaster, and rotting, creaking boards. "Yep, a little paint and we're good as new," he said, fingering a chunk of broken mortar in the living room fireplace.

I was too excited about the bedrooms to notice any imperfections. After nine years of sharing a bedroom with my three brothers, it appeared I was headed for private quarters. There were four bedrooms in the Broadway house. I did the math—a room for my parents, one for my sister, a room for my three brothers, which left one for me. The solitude would be a welcome change.

I was the fourth of five children and was surrounded on all sides by my siblings, whom I loved, despite their eccentricities. The oldest was my sister, Jeanne, whom we called

Chick. My brother Glenn followed her. He was the tallest kid in town and the star of the high school basketball team, helping secure their sole victory in his senior year. Doug was next and was the apple of our mother's eye, owing to an obsessive-compulsive disorder that compelled him to keep our home spotlessly clean. We would have gotten him therapy, had his condition not been so helpful. Then I came along, remarkably free of abnormalities, followed by my brother David, the family artist, who, like many creative types, seemed to suffer inordinately, and was plagued with a spastic colon.

Alas, my wish for solitude would go unmet. When we moved to our Broadway Street home, I would share a bedroom with David. For the next ten years, my nights would be a study in misery, clouds of noxious fumes sucking the air from my lungs, leaving me gasping for breath. As a child, I was slightly built and weak, which I now attribute to David's bodily detonations.

The evening we first visited the Broadway house, we noticed a barn set off to the side, behind the main house. It had a hayloft, a basketball hoop attached to the front, and, wonder of wonders, a stall for a horse, which began our campaign to persuade our parents to buy us one. My father handled our request with consummate skill, dangling the carrot of horse ownership ever before us while extracting a variety of concessions from us over the years. Our quest for a horse eventually took on pathetic dimensions. David began to imagine we actually had a horse, cutting out pictures of horses from magazines, trimming them carefully to fit in his wallet, and showing them to his friends. "This is me in the first grade, here's a picture of my family on vacation, and this is Blackie, my horse."

We moved in on a Saturday in February of 1970. A Red Ball moving van arrived at our old house to load up our earthly belongings, which took roughly ten minutes. Once loaded, the moving van struck out across town, east on Main Street past Danner's Five and Dime, to Tennessee Street, then to Broadway, through a tunnel of trees, and around three corners to our new home. Our family led the procession in our Plymouth Valiant, which had been washed and waxed for the occasion.

The day resides in my memory as the finest of days. It was unseasonably warm, the sky was brilliant, joy and expectancy filled the air. Bluebirds were nearly extinct then, but in my recollections they were thick about us, flitting from tree to tree, heralding our arrival.

Our bicycles had been the last objects loaded on the moving van and so were the first removed. My brothers and I set out to investigate our new surroundings, looping the block, stopping at the Baker Funeral Home to peer through the garage windows to see if there were any dead bodies lying about, but we only saw Rawleigh Baker, the mortician, very much alive, wearing a suit and waxing his hearse.

Our immediate neighbors held little promise for fun and excitement. To our south was Mrs. Draper, a Quaker widow. Catty-corner from us was Mrs. Bryant, another Quaker widow. There were a number of Quaker widows in our neighborhood, who, as near as I could tell, passed their time making quilts they sent out west to cold Indians.

Up the street lived Mr. and Mrs. Norton and their six children, one of whom we called Suds for reasons I no longer remember. Mrs. Norton would sit on the top step of their porch, smoking cigarettes, while her six sticky, feral kids draped themselves across her. The other adults I knew guarded their language when children were present, but Mrs. Norton was a veritable fountain of profanity, and an endless source of fascination to the neighborhood children.

We would sit on her porch, imploring Mrs. Norton for puffs on her cigarette. "What the hell you thinkin'?" she'd say. "You're not old enough. You gotta be at least fifteen."

She would draw deeply from her cigarette, then let the smoke seep out in dribbles while watching the pickup trucks roll past on their way to the dump, which lay a mile south of town so the rich people didn't have to smell their trash.

On Saturday mornings, Mr. Norton would join us on the front step. He never said much. He would sit and listen to his wife, baring his tarry teeth occasionally to grin, then take a deep drag from his cigarette. His hair was neatly combed to a high-rolling pompadour up front and fairly glistened with pomade, which I was afraid would ignite from the cigarette heat. Between the two of them, their home was such a fog even their dog had a smoker's hack. Quite naturally, I was enthralled by the Nortons, they representing everything my mother had ever warned me about.

One fall day, Suds filched a Camel from his father, and he and I smoked it in the woods behind my house, underneath our camping tree. He was a year older than I was, ten, and a veteran smoker. The tips of his fingers were beginning to yellow, and he could blow smoke rings better than Jackie Gleason.

"Don't swallow the smoke," Suds said, passing me the cigarette. "Just suck it in and blow it out."

I smoked half the cigarette, vomited, then lay on my back drawing in fresh air while Suds finished the Camel and made up euphemisms for puking—selling the Buick, ralphing, praying to the porcelain goddess, the Technicolor yawn, driving the bus, and blowing chow. He would cackle after each one. Suds had a mind for metaphors like no one I'd ever known.

The next day, during a game of football, Suds sat on my arm and broke it, and even though I got to wear a cast and it made me a hero at school, I decided the time had come to find more refined company.

I settled on Peanut, so named because of his resemblance to that legume. He was short, curvy, and smooth, and even at the age of nine, nearly bald. Peanut lived around the corner from us. His mother had died when he was little, and his father, unable to care for him, had sent him to Danville to live with relatives. Peanut divided his time between his uncle's house and his grandparents' across town. They were deaf. When their doorbell rang, their lights and television would flicker, announcing company. This was a great attraction to us, and Peanut and I would ring their doorbell several times a day, until his grandfather would come outside and yell at us in sign language.

If Peanut was embarrassed by his nickname, he never let on, and after a while seemed to forget his real name.

When he and I went to register for school, Mrs. Warnock, the school secretary, asked him his name.

"Peanut," he answered.

"I mean your real name," Mrs. Warnock said.

"That is my real name," he said.

"What did your parents name you?" she persisted.

He thought for a moment, then said, "Jeff."

"How do you spell that?"

"P-e-a-n-u-t," he said.

Behind his home was a brick shed, which Peanut told us had been the slaves' quarters when the house was a plantation. The Northwest Ordinance of 1787 had prohibited slavery in Indiana and the house had been built in 1858, but for a kid, Peanut had unusual credibility and we believed him.

Peanut had a cousin named Karen, who I kissed in a game of spin the bottle in the brick shed. When I let it be known we had been romantically involved, she punched me in the nose, and for many years afterward I associated romance with pain.

When we were ten, Peanut and I took part in the Danville Optimist Bicycle Safety Rodeo. I won second-place prize—fifteen dollars and a Salisbury steak dinner at the Westwood Inn, and Peanut won third—ten dollars and a macaroni hotdish. Betty Weesner took our picture for the

Republican newspaper. Ricky White won first place, and several years later leveraged that victory into an appointment to West Point and got his picture hung on the wall at Dave's All-American Pizza and Eatery.

My family had lived in town for thirteen years and had never gotten our picture in the *Republican,* not even a mention in the social column, which you could get just by having your aunt visit or driving to the city for the state fair. But within a year of moving to the rich end of town, we hit the papers and our standing began to build, a portent of the many glories that would eventually come our way. If my mother could have foretold this, I'm sure her initial misgivings about the kitchen ceiling would have dissipated. Instead, she spent the next thirty-four years staring at the water stain, sighing, then looking at Dad and saying, "So when was it you were thinking of fixing that leak?"

Chapter 3

Dreams of Greatness

Danville was (and is) the county seat of Hendricks County. There is a bronze disc in the sidewalk in front of Lawrence's Drugstore, on the east side of the town square, marking the exact center of the county. The spring of my fourth-grade year, Mrs. Conley marched our class two-by-two up Washington Street, where each of us took a turn standing on the disc while she imparted the salient facts concerning our county—founded in 1824, named for then-governor of Indiana, William Hendricks, chief exports included corn, cattle, and mice.

It was an invigorating experience, standing in the exact middle of our county. For a moment, I believed I was in charge of the whole shebang—that I was the governor, the commies had nuked us, and since I was standing on the magic spot, it fell to me to raise our state from the ashes. Then Roydeena Feltner punched me in the shoulder, twice, and told me to move my butt off of there, that it was her turn to stand on the disc.

Mrs. Conley believed in hands-on education and regularly shepherded us about town, pointing out various curiosities—the hackberry tree on the courthouse lawn planted by Union soldiers in 1861; the home of Ira Chase, governor of Indiana from 1891 to 1893, who was content to live with his blind wife in their small home at the corner of Kentucky and Mill streets, wanting nothing to do with the governor's mansion in the city. He rode the train into the city each morning and returned home on the evening train. The governor and his wife had one son, who died when his mother, unable to see the directions, accidentally gave him a fatal dose of medicine. Mrs. Conley wept when she told the story, standing on the sidewalk outside their home, tears glistening on her cheeks like diamonds.

As fascinating as that was, my interest lay in our mouse exports. On the northwest side of town was a long, low building where multitudes of mice were raised in rodent luxury before being trucked to the Eli Lilly factory where they gave their lives for the betterment of our health and welfare. In the winter, when the winds bore down from the northwest, the sweetly pungent odor of mouse droppings settled like a blanket over our town. When the weather fronts had shifted to the south, Mrs. Conley walked us across town to the mousery, explaining the important role the mice played in the eradication of disease and infections, suggesting that if the mousery had been here in the 1890s, the governor's son wouldn't have died. It was a source of unfathomable pride to know our town's mice played a vital role in the elimination of fearsome poxes and blights.

"A lot of our young people go away to college and never return. But this proves," she said, gesturing toward the mousery, "that there are lucrative business opportunities beneficial to mankind right here in Danville."

I would stand on the sidewalk beside Mrs. Conley, whose enthusiasm for mice was contagious. Listening to her discuss the virtues of mice, I dreamed of skipping college altogether and getting hired at the mousery as a turd scooper, then working my way up through the various departments—feeding, insemination, incubation—and on into the gloried reaches of upper management, then starting my own mouse factory and shipping Danville mice all over the world.

It almost happened to Frankie Cunningham, who after high school was hired on to clean the cages at the mousery. By his mid-twenties he was working in the front office as the public relations man. He fielded all the complaints about the mouse smell, able to calm the most irate citizens with his deft humor and cool composure. He was a walking encyclopedia when it came to mice and would leap to their defense when anyone questioned their virtues. I recall when someone within earshot of Frankie made a passing comment about mice, fleas, and the Black Plague.

"With all due respect," Frankie said, ever the diplomat, "the fleas that started the Black Plague were found on black rats, not mice. They're of the same subfamily, *murinae*, but not the same genus, *Rattus rattus* as opposed to *Mus musculus*."

I never knew what the mousery paid Frankie, but he was worth every penny.

Curiously, after years of association with mice, Frankie began to resemble one—white-haired, long whiskers that stood out in straight lines from his face, and two-prominent front teeth that were slightly overbitten. He was heavy on the bottom and his head tapered to a pink point. His looks worked against him; he appeared mistrustful, like a sly rodent. He died a bitter and broken man, infected, ironically, with the hantavirus, after being bitten by a Guatemalan deer mouse.

"Done in by the *Peromyscus guatemalensis*," were his last gasping words.

In addition to selling mice by the millions to Eli Lilly, the mousery also sold them singly to children as pets or snake food. After they got their dime, the people at the mousery seemed coldly indifferent to the mouse's plight. Peanut had a black rat snake he'd caught in the woods behind his house. Each Monday after school, we'd ride our bicycles to the mousery and buy a mouse, which Peanut would carry home in his shirt pocket, its pointy head poking out the top of his pocket, its whiskers plastered back by the wind, grinning, thinking it had broken free, unaware of its fate.

We would drop the mouse into the snake's cage, where it would cower in a corner, its cheerful countenance replaced with one of stark terror. The snake toyed with the mouse, chitchatting with it for several days until it relaxed and reclined in its chair, drinking a Manhattan. The snake would seize hold of it, piercing its neck with its fangs, then swallow it, the mouse's pink little hind legs sticking out of the snake's mouth, kicking frantically.

Because of the ready supply of snake food, serpents were common in our town. Most of the boys had one, and some more than one. They would bring them to Show-and-Tell Day at school, snakes draped around shoulders and sprouting from heads like Medusa's—black rats, corn snakes, king snakes, garden snakes, and hognose snakes lamenting their poor reputation, putting everyone at ease before sinking their fangs in an unsuspecting child's neck, dragging him to the furnace room in the basement and swallowing him whole.

Even so, Mrs. Conley thought the occasional ingestion of a child was a small price to pay, and remained a stout advocate of the mousery, devoting an entire week of our fourth-grade year to extolling its vital role in humanity's advancement. "Never have so many mice suffered so much for so many," she said. She had her students write letters to the state legislature each fall requesting the *Mus musculus* be named the official state mouse, to no avail. We had a state flag, state motto, state flower, state bird, state tree, state stone, state river, state song, state mineral, and even an official state insect—the lightning bug—but no state mouse. It grieved Mrs. Conley to no end. She'd petitioned the school board to change our school's mascot from the Warriors to the Mice, which they declined to do, since Mrs. Kisner, the art teacher, had only recently painted a warrior on the gym floor and was in no mood to replace it with a mouse.

Mrs. Conley was a lonely woman, a visionary in a town of near-sighted people. I wanted to be like her, forward thinking and a leader of people. Each day I would ride my bicycle past Lawrence's Drugstore, dismount, and stand on the bronze disc at the county's center. If my dreams of mousery greatness didn't materialize, my plan B was becoming the governor, riding the train into the city each day as Ira Chase had done, making the *Mus musculus* the official state mouse, then running for the presidency and winning, which Mrs. Conley said could happen to anyone.

"Anyone can be president," she would tell us. I couldn't tell if Mrs. Conley was wildly optimistic or delusional, but it was plain as the nose on your face that not everyone in our class was presidential material. Jerry Sipes was the missing link, a knuckle-dragging mouth breather, strong evidence that the theory of evolution needed further refining. I couldn't imagine any circumstances that might cause a majority of Americans to think Jerry Sipes was the answer to their problems.* Nevertheless, Mrs. Conley persisted in her fantasy. "If you work

* In all fairness, I thought the same thing of George W. Bush.

hard, tell the truth, and get A's on your report card, you too can be president of the United States of America," she said.

Her last requirement eliminated the possibility for me. I was a solid C student in the fourth grade, a middle-of-the-roader, a moderate man, not given to extremes, in search of the middle ground. Plus, I lied a lot. The lying wasn't my fault—the adults in my life left me little choice, peppering me with questions that, had I answered truthfully, would have landed me in hot water.

Adults were always extolling the virtues of honesty, then getting upset when you told the truth.

When Mrs. Conley asked me if I had been the one who'd written the word *phart* on the blackboard, I knew if I told her the truth she'd be disappointed, so I spared her the anguish and lied.

Father McLaughlin asked me every Sunday if I believed Jesus was born of a virgin. I knew if I told the truth, that I had serious doubts, he'd faint dead away, so I said, "You betcha!" and we were both better off.

When Mrs. Conley taught Indiana history, she concluded each lesson by saying, "Now don't you all agree Indiana is the finest state in the nation?" We would nod our heads in agreement, like the little brownnosers we were, even though I preferred Wisconsin. Adults didn't want the truth, so much as they wanted their prejudices confirmed.

Mrs. Conley's class was at the top of the stairs, so when Mrs. Warnock in the office rang the recess bell, we were the first in line for the prime playground equipment. Miss

Stump's class was the last out, and they were stuck with broken swings that pinched their butts and the Slide from Hell. The Slide from Hell rose one hundred feet from the ground. The first week of school, an unsuspecting child, new to our town, would climb to the top, look down, be overcome with vertigo, and plummet to his death. The Slide from Hell was left on the playground as an object lesson about the vicissitudes of life.

Miss Stump, as her name suggested, was squat, round, and unyielding. She drew recess duty while the other teachers smoked cigarettes in the teachers' lounge. She stood watch by the bicycle rack under the maple tree, seething with resentment, scanning the playground for infractions. She would blast her whistle, point to the offending party, and bellow at him to straighten up or else. The *or else* was never defined, though we suspected it had something to do with the creative application of pain, which would be repeated when we got home.*

Mrs. Conley and Miss Stump exhibited the typical views concerning children in those days. Mrs. Conley believed we were destined for greatness, that nothing was beyond our reach. Miss Stump believed prison was too good a fate for us. It was disconcerting to realize Miss Stump had taught more years than Mrs. Conley, indicating that longer exposure to children caused one's opinion of them to lessen.

---

* Every morning, while our mothers were smoothing our cowlicks with mother-spit, our fathers would say, "If you get in trouble at school, you'll get it twice as bad when you get home." I got paddled three times as a child, three whacks per episode. My father owes me eighteen whacks, which he assures me he hasn't forgotten.

Nevertheless, I didn't let this dampen my zeal for life. I knew it was only a matter of time before I would follow in Frankie Cunningham's footsteps and be a leader. First governor, then president by popular demand. Mrs. Conley would be dead by then, but she would look down from heaven and not be surprised by my success. She would be disappointed to know I'd lied about writing the word *phart* on the blackboard—people in heaven knowing everything—but she would have forgiven me, pardon and mercy being required in heaven.

I imagined these future glories and more, standing on the disc at the center of our county, dreaming my wild dreams.

Chapter 4

My Pointless Suffering

According to Mrs. Draper, the Quaker widow next door, my parents were the fifth owners of the Broadway Street house, all of whom had left their mark on it, so it was a curious mix of a place. In addition to that, our relatives showered us with their cast-off furniture and the rooms were soon full, but dissimilar. The front parlors were Victorian, the dining room Colonial, and the living room Daniel Boone-ish with a little '70s decor thrown in for good measure. In all the years my parents lived there, they were never able to synthesize the house into an agreeable whole. Each room had its charms, but none of them harmonized with the others. It was like living in a furniture store, where within a few yards one could find a variety of styles.

The house was not air-conditioned—few of the neighborhood homes were—and so the porch was the center of our lives through the summer. Peanut would arrive each morning after breakfast and sit on our porch swing until we came out.

One morning, I found him studying a small, rounded hole in our front door glass. The origin of the hole was a mystery, although my siblings and I had considered numerous possibilities in the months we had lived there. When I wondered aloud how it could have been made, Peanut peered at it intently, then announced, "Civil War musket ball."

That a Civil War battle hadn't been fought within a hundred miles of Danville, Indiana, didn't alter his opinion. Once Peanut made up his mind about something, the facts could not dissuade him, and he was so persuasive my brothers and I spent the day digging great holes in the yard in search of military relics. We unearthed a long piece of rusted metal that appeared to me to be a discarded lawn mower blade, although Peanut told me I was mistaken and identified it as a sword. "Union Army, I believe. Quite possibly General Grant's."

Besides history, Peanut and I shared other interests, chief among them money and our lack of it. He and I were too young to be employed, so we had to be entrepreneurial and make our own way. For several days we wandered about town picking up empty soda bottles, for which we were reimbursed five cents each at the Kroger store. After two days of work, we had earned a dollar, which we spent on Mexican jumping beans. We charged neighborhood kids a nickel to see them and earned another dollar.

Flush with capital, Peanut suggested we start a newspaper. There were two newspapers in our town, one owned by a Republican and the other by a Democrat. This left the vast Independent market underserved, and Peanut and I resolved to remedy that. My brother David joined us in our venture. He and Peanut went on assignment, interviewing various neighbors and running down hot tips. I was in charge of editing, layout, and production. We named our paper the *Broadway Blab*. It was four pages, and when there weren't enough true stories to fill it, we resorted to rumor and innuendo, which caused the circulation to skyrocket to its peak of twenty-five homes. We wrote the paper in longhand and soon were too busy writing to go in search of news and had to invent it out of whole cloth. In our fourth week, we wrote an exposé on Quaker widows, alienated our base, and had to cease operations.

My economic well-being in jeopardy, I asked my parents for an allowance.

"Sure," my father said. "Tell you what we'll do. If you mow the yard, make your bed, keep your bedroom clean, sweep out the barn, carry out the trash, and do the supper dishes, we'll give you a place to sleep, clothes to wear, and food to eat."

This was my father's customary response to my requests for an allowance.

"James Martin gets an allowance," I pointed out. "Two dollars a week."

James Martin lived up the street and bought his clothes at Beecham's Menswear on the square, instead of at yard sales like the rest of us. He hailed from serious money.

"We're not the Martins," my father said.

That was abundantly clear.

The next week, I walked past the Martin's house and saw three men, dressed in white uniforms, painting their house. James was playing in his side yard.

"Who are those guys?" I asked.

"My dad hired them to paint our house," he said.

I stood on the sidewalk, grappling with that foreign idea. Hiring someone to work on your house! That's when I knew the Martins were class.

When our house had been built in 1913, a number of handymen would hire themselves out for a modest sum, but by 1970 their ranks had dwindled to one Hiram Bybee, who'd been bitten on the chin by a bat, gone mad in the head, and was wildly unpredictable. So the home repairs fell to my father, who, though not accomplished with tools, was well thought of and able to persuade friends and neighbors to help, usually by plying them with beer. Within a few years, our home was wallpapered, the kitchen renovated, porch roofed, barn painted, fence erected, and roof leaks plugged.

Three of the more colorful volunteers were the Lofton brothers—Mitch, Ronnie, and Jake—whom my father had met in his line of work, selling bug spray to grocery stores throughout Indiana. I would stand off to the side, watching the men work, fetching tools and beer, whatever they required. The beer tended to animate the Lofton brothers, and as the day progressed their inhibitions would lessen, as did the quality of their work. Shingles went on upside down, fences ran crooked, entire sections of barn were left unpainted. Any woman walking past was scrutinized, possible liaisons suggested. I found our encounters with the Lofton brothers thrilling, every bit as interesting as the Buckhorn Bar, but it distressed my brother David, who would stalk through the house, a pubescent Jeremiah, a weeping prophet, predicting their damnation.

Even with such able assistance, the house was a jealous mistress, demanding every spare moment of Dad's time. He worked long hours selling bug spray, so many of the regular chores fell to my siblings and me, and we quickly became adept at avoiding them. Indeed, if we had devoted as much thought and energy to work as we did to evading it, our house would have been a showcase. Because we didn't, it was a curiosity, a reference point against which others could measure their decline.

The situation came to a head each October, when the numerous trees on our three-acre lawn shed staggering amounts of leaves. Before my father left for work, he would say, "I want those leaves raked by the time I get home." It was an absurd request, biblical in proportion, similar to Pharaoh's order that the Israelites make bricks without straw. Our rakes were gap-toothed, missing most of the tines. The few remaining prongs were bent at odd angles. My dad would compound matters by purchasing one new rake each fall, which my brothers and I would fight over like refugees scrapping for a crust of bread.

Our friends deserted us in droves during October, lest they be drawn into our misery. Even Peanut, who was usually unflagging in his support, forsook us in October to play with James Martin, whose father had a leaf sweeper he pulled behind a riding mower. One October, while the Martins were gone, my brother Glenn made off with their sweeper. Lacking a riding mower, we hitched it to our brother Doug, who pulled it back and forth across the yard, leaving clean green stripes in his wake. We had all the leaves picked up and the sweeper returned before anyone was the wiser. We would have gotten away with it, except Suds Norton ratted us out and we had to apologize to the Martins and act like we were sorry, even though we weren't.

For as long as my siblings and I lived at home, my father refused to buy a riding lawn mower. My brothers and I mowed the lawn with a push mower whose right front tire would work loose and fall off.* Dad refused to upgrade, believing irrational hardship strengthened one's moral fiber. He had a number of interesting theories about character development, most of them involving tedious labor and pointless suffering.

This perspective was not unique to my father. Other men of his generation, born in the thick of the Great Depression, seemed positively giddy about adversity. They were especially fond of war, and regularly suggested it as the cure for what ailed us. Since Vietnam was stumbling to an end with no other war on the horizon, home maintenance became the front on which I was tested and found wanting.

* My sister, Chick, being a girl, never mowed the lawn. It simply wasn't done.

This battle took the following, predictable patterns:

Me: Say, Dad, I was at Norton's the other day, and noticed their rakes had tines on them. Maybe we could get one of those.

Dad: Why, when I was your age, we didn't even have rakes. We had to pick up leaves with our bare hands.

Or—

Me: Boy, I sure wish our lawn mower had four wheels.

Dad: Why, when I was little, our lawn mower only had two wheels. Maybe if you'd been to war, you'd have a little more gumption.

It soon became apparent that I had a gumption deficit. Roydeena Feltner was in my grade and lived three blocks west of us. Every morning, on my way to school, she punched me in the shoulder and called me a pansy. I began taking my dog Zipper to school with me, for protection. But Roydeena gave her a Milk-Bone, then slugged me. When I hit Roydeena back, Zipper bit me.

Nevertheless, I liked to imagine I had gumption. One day, when I was around eleven, my father pulled in the driveway bearing a large carton of orange backpacks adorned with pictures of bugs breathing their last after being doused with bug spray. Dad, by virtue of his vocation, could always be depended upon to furnish us with the most curious items having to do with bugs—bug backpacks, bug telephones, bug radios, bug shirts, bug hats, and bug wristwatches.

The bug backpack was my favorite. I would fill it with camping gear, then strike out into the wild behind our house with Peanut in tow. We'd hike to the camping tree, build a fire, open a can of Dinty Moore beef stew with the lumberjack on the label, cook it over the coals, then eat it straight from the can. Gumption food.

Hiking back, I pretended we were returning home from the Civil War, that we'd been gone four years fighting the cursed Rebels, and that the rest of my family, without me there to protect them, had been attacked and killed by Indians, leaving me to figure out the meaning of it all and carry on without them. But my family was always fine and going about their business. Indeed, they seemed unaware I'd even been gone from home, let alone to war.

"Your father wants you to mow the lawn," my mother said, by way of greeting.

The task of mowing fell to me and my brother Doug. The rest of us kids first noticed his obsessive-compulsiveness when he was ten years old and began vacuuming the living room carpet without being told. We knew then he had a serious problem—none of us ever did anything without being asked to. But Doug seemed to enjoy the work, guiding the vacuum cleaner back and forth across the room in precise lines, demanding that everyone walk with the nap and not against it.

He was equally neurotic about the lawn, so when it was my turn to mow, I would careen across the yard, pushing the mower in a crooked, noodley line, which he could not tolerate. He would burst from the house, waving his arms, shouting at me to stop, and then wrest the mower from me and take over, mowing my section and his in clean right angles to the street. We had the neatest lawn in town and people used to drive by just to see it.

David, the youngest, was the last of the siblings to leave home. The day after he moved, my father drove to Sears and bought a riding mower, a stunning violation of his gumption-development theory. If I still published the *Broadway Blab*, I would expose that and other lies I was told were necessary for my well-being. Instead, I pass these untruths down to my sons, in hopes they will one day be examples of self-sufficiency and gumption, like their father and grandfather before them.

Chapter 5

Big Business

My dreams for success came to a head in the fifth grade, when a Mrs. Louise Moffat visited our school, gave a rousing oration on the benefits of free enterprise, then urged my classmates and me to consider a lucrative career in newspaper delivery. Her speech was a masterpiece of psychological manipulation, appealing to our desire for money while taking full advantage of our ignorance. She promised obscene riches for little effort—"Make ten, twenty, yes, even thirty dollars a week for minutes of fun each day!" This seemed vastly superior to working for my dad, who didn't pay me anything, so I enrolled on the spot, and was given the assignment of delivering the *Indianapolis News* to twenty-six households on the south side of town.

This was back in the days before child labor laws, when employers could exploit children for financial gain, making all sorts of promises they had no intention of keeping, driving children to wrack and ruin, while the parents united in telling their kids it was for their own good.

I was required to deliver the newspaper wearing a yoked bag over my shoulders, emblazoned with the phrase the *Indianapolis News* on one side and the *Great Hoosier Daily* on the other. The bag could only be rented, not purchased, and so I labored in a state of indentured servitude, up to my eyeballs in hock for bag rental, paying tenfold more than its value. The real profit for the *Indianapolis News* lay not in selling newspapers, but in renting bags to its carriers.

What the job lacked in financial gain, it made up for in camaraderie. Bill Eddy and Bunny Runyan had also fallen prey to Louise Moffat's pitch and joined me in the venture. Bunny Runyan was the only kid I ever knew to make money delivering newspapers. He carried a thick wad of bills in his front pocket. We never figured out how he did it, and he never told. Bunny became Louise Moffat's poster boy of newspaper success. Whenever we complained about being cheated, she would point to Bunny's financial success, which always reduced us to grudging silence. I now believe Louise Moffat was salting the mine, slipping Bunny an extra twenty bucks a week in order to seduce the rest of us with prospects of prosperity.

Louise Moffat played us like a cheap violin. Whenever we were on the verge of uprising, she would announce a free trip to the Kings Island amusement park near Cincinnati to those carriers who signed up five new customers in the next week. We would temporarily forget all our hardships and respond with a frenzy, striking out in search of new subscribers to the *Great Hoosier Daily*.

I was so easily manipulated, I would probably still be delivering newspapers if Peanut hadn't broken the spell Louise Moffat had over me. I'd spent an entire Saturday trying to drum up new customers, had failed miserably, and was thoroughly dejected.

"All you have to do is make up five names and addresses," Peanut said. "She probably never checks on them, so long as their bill gets paid. Then when you get back from Kings Island, tell her they all moved away. It's simple."

I did the arithmetic in my head. The newspaper cost sixty cents a week, which meant that for a modest investment of three dollars, I could visit Kings Island. Not wanting to keep this fine secret to myself, I told all the other carriers and we banded together to stick it to Louise Moffat and the *Great Hoosier Daily*, with the exception of Doreena Waltrip, the only girl carrier, who said God would strike us dead and send us to hell for cheating. It turns out she was mistaken; we didn't go to hell, we went to Kings Island.

The week after we returned, a number of cancellations were reported. A scandal ensued, Mrs. Moffat was transferred, and a Mr. Strunk took her place. He promptly did away with such pleasantries as trips, increased our bag rental, and set out to bring us under his cigarette-yellowed thumb. Though the carriers had won the battle, the newspaper had won the war, and we resigned ourselves to further depravations, except for Doreena Waltrip, who was given the paper route where the big tippers lived.

Collection day was Thursday. Most of my customers were elderly women on Social Security who paid me in pennies they'd found under the cushions of their couches. They would count them out, one by one, into my hand, then recount them, just to be sure they hadn't given me too much. By the end of the day, I wanted to rip their blue hair out by the roots.

The upside of the job was the girlie calendar in the back room of Mooney's TV and Radio. The first day of the month, the calendar was turned to a new girlie and a swarm of deviants would gather at the rear window to watch her unveiling. Everyone else had to view the calendar from twenty feet away through a grimy window, but every Thursday, on collection day, I would enter the back room, where Mr. Mooney was fixing TVs, and sneak glances at that month's featured attraction.

The calendar relied heavily on the male imagination. Vital parts weren't bared, so much as hinted at, but this was typical of sex education in my adolescence—short on specifics and long on speculation. I was eleven when I first heard the word *vagina*, and even then I thought it had something to do with chest pain. Until then, reproductive organs had been referred to as privates, plumbing, down there, and winkie.

Scotty Blake, another carrier, was eleven, smoked, and knew everything there was to know about women. His mother was a nurse and had taught him all the words, which he passed on to the rest of us. Today, he'd probably be arrested, but back then he entertained large audiences of boys with his insights on the feminine mystique. Kids like Scotty would eventually cause parents to homeschool their children.

The newspaper station was near the bus stop, in the basement beneath Dr. Heimansohn's dental office. The bus from Indianapolis would idle at the corner, diesel fumes belching out and spilling into the basement, gassing the carriers like rats. We would swarm up the stairs, haul the stacks of newspapers from the cargo space underneath the bus, carry them down to the basement, fold them, then go on our way, dubious ambassadors for the *Great Hoosier Daily*.

Mr. Strunk was a stickler for public opinion, insisting we be neatly groomed, punctual, and polite. Delivering papers was like going to church every day. It had been our custom to play pinball at the Danner's Five and Dime while waiting for the bus to bring the papers out from the city, but Mr. Strunk brought that sordid custom to a screeching halt. "You are not hoodlums. You represent the finest newspaper in the finest state in the finest country in the world. Act like it!"

Fascism holds a certain appeal for the morally rigid, and Doreena Waltrip swooned at Mr. Strunk's every utterance. Doreena attended a fundamentalist church in our town and devoted much of her time to getting Scotty Blake right with the Lord. Initially, he resisted, which heightened her determination.

She had his name placed in her church's newsletter, in the Needs Saving column. Scotty was resistant to salvation, but as Doreena began to bud into womanhood, his interest in spiritual matters deepened, and he had further discussions with her, listening carefully while she fleshed out the finer points of faith. He seemed particularly intrigued with Doreena's belief that once you were saved you could pretty much do anything you wanted and God still had to let you into heaven.

"So what you're saying," he asked her one afternoon, clearly trying to put ideas into her head, "is that people who aren't married, maybe even someone our age, can do it and still go to heaven."

Even Scotty Blake didn't use the word *sex* in mixed company, employing the word *it* instead.

Doreena had been backed into a theological corner and knew it. "Yes," she said, "but true Christians wouldn't do that."

"But if they had a moment of weakness and did it, God would forgive them. Right?"

"If they'd prayed the sinner's prayer, God would forgive them," Doreena said.

"Well, praise the Lord!" Scotty said. "Let's pray."

And right there, amidst the fog of diesel fumes, Scotty Blake found the Lord. Unfortunately, he proved to be an indifferent disciple, rigorously testing the limits of God's forgiveness, and after a while even Doreena Waltrip gave up on him.

It was Scotty Blake, who, after we carriers were banned from the Five and Dime, told us about the *Police Gazette*, sold at the Rexall drugstore, which showed pictures of crime victims in various states of undress. This made for fascinating reading. Crimes were a rarity in our town, especially those involving scantily clad women. For that matter, scantily clad women were also uncommon. Ours was a discreet populace, a God-fearing people who shunned nudity unless we were bathing or Dr. Kirtley had to check us for hernias. Rumors of nudity were circulated and dwelled upon, but never proven.

Scotty Blake used this adolescent lust to his advantage when Mr. Strunk, facing a carrier shortage, offered us five dollars for every new carrier we recruited. Scotty concocted stories of lonely housewives, dressed in skimpy negligees, answering the door on collection day and inviting the paperboy inside, resulting in an influx of new carriers and earning Scotty fifty dollars and the Carrier of the Year Award.

It seems odd now to think that a good portion of my puberty was spent meditating on naked women. I can only attribute such perversity to a massive surge of hormones, an evolutionary leftover, nature's way of continuing the species. Of course, now I know that nudity and lust are sins, causing all manner of problems, chief among them acne and blindness.

Chapter 6

Vacations

As bug spray salesmen go, my father was unsurpassed. Several times a year he'd come home lugging a prize from a sales contest—a television, transistor radio, clock, set of steak knives, or coffee mug. One memorable spring he won a family camping package—tent, sleeping bags, Coleman cookstove, and a Ray-O-Vac flashlight—so for several summers we vacationed at Lane's Camping Retreat near Spencer, Indiana. My dad had discovered the campground on his bug route and had bartered with the owner for a week of camping in exchange for five cases of mosquito repellant.

During the heat of the day, we'd pile in the car and drive to Spencer, to the Moss and Money Drug Store where we would sit at the soda fountain and eat ice cream. My dad would pay the bill in bottles of aftershave, which his company had recently added to its line of merchandise. The aftershave was a by-product of the manufacture of piney woods–scented bug spray. "For years, we just threw it away," he told me. "Then we noticed it smelled nice, so we put it in glass bottles and sold it as aftershave. Plus, it keeps the bugs away. Can't beat that with a stick."

With the expansion of its product line, my father's company was prospering, and the next summer we were given an all-expenses paid trip to Lac du Flambeau, Wisconsin, near the headwaters of the great Turtle River on the shores of Fence Lake. The camp was owned by the bug spray company my father worked for and consisted of a dozen small cabins huddled beside the lake, a picnic table outside each one, speckled with the remnants of fish cleaning—blood and guts and scales.

The cabin had two bedrooms. My parents took one and put us five children in the other. David, then ten, had to sleep in a baby's crib. Naturally, my brothers and I ridiculed him mercilessly and the experience warped him for life.

The cabin reeked of fish past and was decorated in a fish motif—fish pictures, fish mounted on the walls, fish plates, fish blankets, fish salt-and-pepper shakers. We were up to our gills in fish. My father loved to fish and spent most of the week in the boat, catching thousands of fish, which he cleaned on the picnic table and fried in a cast-iron skillet three times a day.

Midway through the week, we drove into Lac du Flambeau, where my parents bought each of us kids a pair of genuine moccasins, hand stitched by Chippewa Indians. I purchased a Boy Scout knife that had a can opener, screwdriver, bottle opener, leather punch, and knife blade. I'd begged for a knife for years, but my mother had refused, predicting all manner of catastrophes that would befall me if I owned one—inadvertent amputations, death by bloodletting, and the severing of the optic nerve. But this time my mother, her brain function impaired by close confinement with five loud children, gave her assent. "Just don't get blood on your new moccasins," she warned. Blood on clothing was a passionate concern of hers. I could sever an aorta, my blood fountaining in the air, splashing on my clothes, and my mother would have been screaming, "Use cold water, not hot. Cold water!"

The knife came in a pouch that I wore on my belt. To this day, I recall the delicious heft of that knife, how the feel of it at my side emboldened me. I dreamed of being attacked by a bear in the Wisconsin woods and killing it with my knife, then skinning it with the can opener blade, draping its pelt across my shoulders, and returning home to great acclaim for my courage. But the bears didn't cooperate, and I settled for spending the rest of the vacation next to the soda machine at the lodge, removing the caps from bottles of pop.

Underneath the camp's bucolic veneer, tension was building. It was 1972 and rumors of a federal ban on DDT were sweeping the bug spray camp. At night, the men would gather at the lodge to play poker and curse the Environmental Protection Agency. Loyal Republicans, ardent supporters of Richard Nixon, and here he was acting like a communist and banning DDT. What a betrayal!

"You get a few birds being born with three wings, so they're gonna outlaw DDT. Whadda they gonna do when kids start dropping dead from the typhoid?" Big Ed Danowski asked. "They think the Black Plague was bad, they ain't seen nothin' yet."

Big Ed Danowski, his wife, and their son, Little Ed, hailed from Racine, Wisconsin, and were staying in the cabin next to ours. Big Ed was a legend in the bug spray business, selling mosquito repellant across the upper Great Lakes region. He could see his bug spray empire crashing to the ground.

We children were oblivious to this pending disaster and passed most of our time making fun of one another and swimming. The camp had an activities director named Art, who'd been hired to oversee the children, but spent most of his time with the mothers. He wore tight shorts and a muscle shirt and taught the women how to shoot bows and arrows by standing behind them, his arms around their bodies, his strong hands encompassing theirs, waves of piney-woods aftershave rolling off his body. One afternoon it rained, so we stayed indoors and Art gave a lecture on Indian lore and revealed that he was one-quarter Chippewa, which caused the women to swoon.

While Art was doing all he could to take our minds off the looming DDT fiasco, the men were fishing and bad-mouthing him behind his back. They detested Art.

On the last morning of our Wisconsin vacation, Art dug a deep hole behind the lodge, lit a fire in it, then set a cast-iron pot of beans in the hole and covered it with earth. It was, he informed us, an old Indian trick. That night my brothers Glenn and Doug gorged themselves on undercooked beans and suffered gas the entire trip home. Thirteen hours in a closed-up car, running on fumes, thanks to Art. By the time we reached Danville, the pine tree air freshener hanging from the rear view mirror had exhausted itself, wilting to a dead brown and shedding its cardboard needles.

Like most vacations, the years imparted a certain charm to that one, and now we look back on our week with Art with great fondness. My father's company survived the ban on DDT and even flourished, branching into shaving cream, window cleaner, and furniture polish, although we remember the glory days of DDT, when Big Ed Danowski and other men of vision moved from one triumph to another.

We continued to prosper and my father hinted at the possibility of international travel the following summer. By international travel, we assumed he meant London or Paris and for several winter months we talked of little else. Dad held his cards close to his chest, not revealing the destination, only promising it would be the finest vacation we'd ever taken. One evening in June, after school had let out for the summer, he assembled our family in the dining room and unveiled his plans. He rolled out a map of Ontario on the table and pointed to the town of Madoc, on the rugged shores of Lake

Weslemkoon. (*Weslemkoon*, we later learned, was an Indian word that translated roughly to "black flies the size of eagles.")

"We're going fishing!" he exclaimed.

"Fishing?" my mother said, visions of Paris dying in her head.

"Wait, it gets better." My father paused for effect. "We're staying on an island in a cabin. We'll be the only ones on the whole island. It's wilderness country up there." He turned to my mother. "The closest town is thirty miles away, so you'll need to make sure we take everything we need."

"What about toilets?" my brother Glenn asked. Since the days of Adam, members of my family have been stricken with spastic colons. Proximity to restrooms has been a prominent consideration in our travels for as long as I can remember.

"Not to worry," my father said. "There's a two-holer behind the cabin."

It was 710 miles from Danville to the grocery store in Madoc—a long, quiet ride that we spent contemplating having to poop into an open pit.

The Madoc grocery store was owned by a Chinese man named Richard who didn't speak English. He was, however, fluent in French, an ironic reminder of our dashed vacation dreams. We arranged our supplies in the car, then drove north on a gravel road thirty miles to the Lake Weslemkoon marina, where we donned life jackets and were conveyed to the island in a wooden boat captained by a grizzled veteran of many crossings. Rendered mute by our circumstances, we clutched the gunwales while great clouds of black flies and mosquitoes swarmed around us.

My father's valor stands out in my memory. Perched in the prow of the boat, the wind in his face, his eyes scanning the horizon, he was Admiral Nelson sailing toward Trafalgar. "Land ho," he cried out, when the island appeared off our starboard side. "Brace yourself for the landing!"

The boatman pulled alongside the dock, helped us lift out the supplies, then said, "Be back for you next Friday. No way to get in touch with anybody, so be careful. Couple summers back, we dropped off a man who lopped his foot off with an ax." He took the pipe from his mouth and pointed it toward the cabin, smiling at the memory. "Bled to death on the front porch. Very first day. Hadn't even unpacked his bags. No tellin' how long it took him to die. Well, enjoy yourselves."

My mother promptly confiscated my pocketknife.

The cabin, though rustic, was also lacking in amenities, including electricity, a shortcoming the cabin's owners had failed to mention. Several of the interior walls were blackened by past fires, begun, we speculated, by kerosene lanterns hanging on the walls. The cabin was nearly fifty years old, the logs cracked and paper dry, on the verge of spontaneous combustion. A dead animal smell pervaded the place.

We raised the screenless windows to air the place out; mosquitoes and black flies buzzed into the cabin. "Would you look at the size of those flies!" my father said, beside himself with joy. He opened a case of bug spray, and began dousing the cabin, moving from room to room, leaving a fog of poison in his wake. My father was a consummate killer of insects, able to pluck from his stores of pesticides the one spray that would ensure a bug's hasty demise. Ants, roaches, termites, gnats, or mosquitoes—each pest was especially vulnerable to a particular toxin, and my father knew it, how best to apply it, and in what amount. Indeed, he was consumed with the topic of bug eradication, and while reading advice columns in the *Great Hoosier Daily*, would comment that what newspapers needed was a daily column on insect extermination. My father took his bugs seriously.

Chick soon tracked down the source of the dead animal smell—a family of mice, clustered in the fireplace, huddled around the charcoal remnants of a fire. They appeared to have frozen to death. Their tails had cracked off, their eyes rolled back in their mouse heads, their front legs crossed about their chests in a vain effort to preserve their body heat. They looked like Ned Beatty in *Deliverance*, shriveled and stricken, their retreat to the wilderness gone awry. We were not encouraged.

By then it was supper time, we were hungry with few prospects for nourishment. We had beef jerky, apples, and Tang, the drink of astronauts!* It is possible, but not pleasant, to live for years on beef jerky, apples, and Tang. Dinner was a quiet affair. We gummed our jerky, reducing it to

* Beef jerky, for the uninformed, is a thin, overcooked piece of cow, possessing the texture and consistency of wood. Impervious to stomach acid, it passes through the digestive tract unchanged and has been known to obstruct bowels for weeks. It is also useful for patching shoes and tires, and in a pinch can be used for weather stripping.

wads small enough to swallow, pausing every now and then to wash it down with Tang.

Most of our time was spent fishing, there being precious little else to do. Lake Weslemkoon, it turns out, enjoyed some fame as a bass lake. The week we were there, my father caught bass as big as dolphins, pulling in one in after another, a veritable orgy of angling. He left the cabin early each morning and wasn't seen again until late in the day, staggering home under a load of bass, which my mother fried over a fire.

By the third day, we had lost all semblance of civility. The lake was too cold to swim in, and lacking running water, we reeked of wood smoke and fish. We hadn't brushed our teeth in days; our breath smelled like dead mice. We ate with our fingers, grubbing through piles of fish bones, picking them clean, snarling and snapping at anyone who approached our food. Wanting to steer clear of the outhouse, my brothers and I had been peeing in the lake, only to discover, near the end of our time there, that the water for our Tang had come straight from our pee place.

We didn't go anywhere for several years, then memories of past agonies faded and we decided to give it another go. Once again, fishing was our vacation theme. We drove 408 mind-numbing miles to the Lake of the Ozarks near Osage Beach, Missouri. My mother navigated, reading the directions aloud to my father. Like the cabins at Lac du Flambeau, these were owned by the bug spray company that employed my father. I now believe the Ozark camp was an experimental proving ground for their bug poisons. The cabin we were assigned was infested with every insect known to man—African fire ants, cockroaches, centipedes, millipedes, water bugs, beetles, and some type of great fanged spider I'd never seen, and haven't seen since.

We pulled up to the cabin, which looked like something out of Appalachia. Sagging and leaning, collapsing into itself, I half expected to see a gaggle of slack-jawed, cross-eyed Snuffy Smiths peering out the windows, their fingers caressing the triggers of their shotguns.

"Oh, dear," my mother said. "Surely this is a mistake."

Dad studied the directions. "Nope. We're at the right place. Say, would you look at that lake!"

We stayed an entire week, seven days too long. Doug was stricken with an ear infection so severe the contagion leaked into his brain and he spent the week in a fevered daze, out of his gourd, pus oozing from every orifice.

The opportunities for nonfishing recreation were few. There was a recreation center, which had a pool table with ripped felt, plus an air hockey machine that stole our quarters without giving us a game. On the fifth day, my ordinarily rational mother lost fifty cents in the air hockey machine. With a quiet, controlled fury she began pounding the machine until the security guard—a densely-pimpled young man—threatened to arrest her. David and I watched from behind the pool table, yelling at the guard, our family's descent into Jerry Springer madness full and complete.

That night we attended a carnival where Chick befriended the Tilt-A-Whirl man and went for a loop with him on the Ferris wheel. We stood beneath the Ferris wheel, craning our necks, peering to the top. Our cultural sensibilities had become so warped in the space of a week that the prospect of marriage between my sister and the Tilt-A-Whirl man seemed a grand idea.

"Chick always did want to travel," my father said cheerfully. "If she marries a carnival man, she can see the world."

My mother nodded in agreement, smiling at her daughter's immense good fortune, imagining the joy of Jethro Bodine grandchildren.

We children clustered about them, eating deep-fried Twinkies, our teeth green with LimeAde.

Providentially, a family emergency—an inadvertent family pregnancy—caused us to be summoned home before all our senses were dulled.

That fall my brother Glenn would go to college, and our family vacations drew to an end. The birds launched from the nest one by one, headed to the horizons, and were never able to be gathered for one last trip. But every now and then, an unbidden memory of those sylvan days comes to mind, a snapshot pasted in the album of memory—woods running down to the lake that was as wet in my recollections as it was in real life.

Chapter 7

My Family Tree, Imagined and Otherwise

My mother's people were Belgian glassworkers who washed up on America's shores in the early 1900s, when the Old Country, thick with kaisers and kings and their attendant tiffs, was proving to be an inhospitable land. My father's people had arrived centuries before, four Quaker brothers who'd landed in North Carolina in the late 1600s. By 1913 our branch had taken up with the Baptists, settled in southern Illinois, and were working the coal mines. My grandfather Gulley, watching his father and uncles emerge from the earth coughing up tarry sputum and dying young, took up sales.

I do not recall my grandfather. He died when I was a year old. His estate was modest, and I only inherited two things—a birdhouse and his disdain of closed-in spaces. My will contains strict instructions that I am to be cremated, a last visit to the cosmic woodstove, the fire's heat warming my rickety bones one more time. It is against my every instinct to be six feet under, ensconced in cement, a lid of steel scant inches from my nose, the air close and basement damp, the worms and rust consuming.

My Illinois kin passed most of their daylight underground, picking away at coal, then crawling out and spending the remaining hours outside, sitting in scalloped metal chairs in their backyards, the western sun soaking into their bones, building up a reservoir of light against the next day's gloom. We visited them every summer, driving the four hours to Valier, Illinois, where our relatives lived in a row—Gulleys, Mackeys, Brownings, and Genesios. Everyone in town was related to us, connected by generations of liaisons, some recognized by the church, others not. Feuds from the 1920s were as fresh as yesterday.

"Your great-grandmother Gulley and your great-grandmother Mackey had a fistfight there," my great-uncle Johnny told me, some fifty years later, pointing to a spot in the street. "I was six years old, and Mrs. Gulley had a new electric washer and yelled across the street to Mrs. Mackey that she was too poor to have an electric washer. They met right there in the middle of the street, slapping and scratching and pulling hair."

Decades later, he was still embarrassed by it. "But we don't talk about it," he said.

"Then what happened?" I persisted, knowing the most interesting topics were the ones people were loathe to discuss.

"Well, Mrs. Gulley's son married Mrs. Mackey's daughter, that would be your grandparents, and things worked themselves out."

When my grandmother wrote her memoir, she left out the story of her mother and mother-in-law duking it out on the streets of Valier and simply noted, "Both our families were pleased with the union."

There is no humiliation so deep that can't be remedied with a little public relations.

Whenever we visited Valier, the women would reside in the refined luxury of my aunt Hazel's home, while the males stayed at our cousin Pooner's house. Pooner was married to Barbara, a small, nervous woman always at the ready, awaiting the slightest hint from Pooner that he might need something. "Do you want some iced tea?" she'd ask him hourly. "How about some chicken, honey? Want me to fry up a chicken?"

Pooner would smile, nod his head, then rattle the ice in his near-empty glass, his signal that the tea situation was getting dire.

Our relatives in Valier ate chicken morning, noon, and night. Great plates of brown, crusty, fried chickens, necks freshly wrung, who just the day before had been in ignorant chicken bliss, scratching in the dirt and eating bugs, unaware of their fate.

After a while, my relatives came to resemble chickens—heavy on the top with chicken-like legs, fleet of foot. They ran races in Pooner's side yard. Cousins and uncles, well into their fifties, lining up, pawing at the ground, straining at the bit, then bursting from the blocks and running, their arms pumping, crossing the finish line, then strutting about the yard, struggling mightily to disguise their shortness of breath. These men were in heart attack country and the nearest hospital with a cardiac unit was in Carbondale, thirty miles down Highway 51. Their wives would pace back and forth on the sidelines, wringing their hands.

Barbara would take Pooner by the hand and lead him to a lawn chair. "How about a chicken?"

The children would also race—my brothers and I and our cousin thrice-removed, Lori, whom I secretly loved, but knew I couldn't marry because we would have deformed children, little ankle-biters with three chicken legs.

On our last night at Pooner's we would dispense with the chicken and drive to the next town to the Maid-Rite and eat hamburgers and drink flat Coke in Styrofoam cups. On the way back we would stop at my cousin David's, who lived in a yellow house that had a pool. While we swam, the adults would sit by the pool and visit. That evening, my father would take his annual swim, mounting the diving board, his stomach glowing white in the moonlight, then swan dive into the deep end and swim the length and back underwater. It was amazing to watch, my father slipping gracefully into the water with scarcely a ripple. He would reminisce about diving in the 1956 Olympics, which we believed, since he was our father and would never lie to us.

My father's participation in sports was limited to one grand exhibit each year—one dive, one basketball shot, one pitch—each of them spectacular. Every fall, when our neighborhood basketball season was well under way, he would emerge from the house, stand at the edge of our gravel court, forty feet from the hoop attached to the front of the barn. He would clap his hands for the basketball, bounce it three times, no more, no less, then heave the ball in a high arc toward the basket and cleanly through it. He would turn and walk back in the house, never speaking a word. In baseball, it was always one pitch, blazing fast and right down the pipe. And that one poetic swan dive at my cousin David's each summer. We could have sold tickets.

This dramatic flair was typical of the men in my family. They could rise to any occasion, but only once. Sustained excellence had never been their strong suit. They hit it big in their youth, peaking early, which gave them something to talk about the rest of their lives. Each summer they would gather under the maple trees in Pooner's backyard and relive their past glories, many of them having to do with elaborate pranks they'd pulled off in their heady days of youth. They would wheeze with laughter, their round sides heaving in and out, recalling things they'd done that would have gotten their offspring grounded for life.

I looked forward to our annual visits to Valier and was especially fascinated by Pooner, who had a number of hobbies and indulged them with an unequaled fervor, embracing one pastime after another, never doing anything halfway. When he took up fishing, he had a pond built in the field behind his house. When his wife expressed an interest in sewing, he added a sewing annex to their home. Then came golf, and he had a driving range installed. After muskrats weakened the dam on his pond, he took up varmint control, purchasing a wide assortment of armament, most of it conventional, but some that wasn't, including what I now suspect were tactical nuclear weapons. Pooner was never one to let the customary constraints of money or law dampen his enthusiasm. Since the other adults we knew valued moderation and restraint, we children were inordinately fond of Pooner, knowing he could always be depended upon to be interesting.

Pooner's little brother, Clarence, father of Lori, lived next door to Pooner and Barbara. Clarence owned the only Harley-Davidson motorcycle in town and consequently served as the town's volunteer policeman, with the authority to arrest anyone he wanted for the slimmest of reasons. He would take us for rides through town on his Harley, looking for ne'er-do-wells to incarcerate. Clarence was a rogue male, a bull elephant; he kept girlie magazines in his bathroom, which led to an outbreak of colonic activity among my brothers and me, requiring frequent trips to the restroom.

At its peak, Valier had roughly seven hundred residents, a grocer, a hardware store, a Gulf gas station, Pinky's candy store, and an auto body shop. My second cousin Virginia had married a man named Barney, who served as the school superintendent in the neighboring town. Virginia and Barney were our family's success story. They lived in a brick ranch house, had a dishwasher, garbage disposal, and bought a new car every two years. The rest of the family was eating their dust.

Barney was too dignified to run footraces. He would sit in the scalloped metal chair in his suit and tie, his hair neatly combed, the embodiment of dignity. His father, Pinky, had owned the candy store, and was well regarded until he put a pool table in the back room of the store and was placed on every prayer list in town. Methodists, Baptists, Pentecostals, and Presbyterians laid aside their differences to unite on the one thing they could agree—that Pinky Genesio was headed straight to hell.

My dad was in awe of Barney Genesio and pointed to him as the archetype of excellence. "That Barney Genesio, he's really something. Probably the greatest man in our family. It's a great family that can give the world a Barney Genesio," my father would say whenever Barney's name was mentioned. Technically, our family had not produced Barney. He had married into us, but this was a genealogical nicety my father was willing to overlook. Indeed, my dad often adopted famous persons into our family, declaring them to be great-great uncles or third cousins or some other distant relation.

I grew up convinced I was the great-great nephew of Alvin C. York, the World War I hero and Medal of Honor winner, whom the movie *Sergeant York* portrayed, starring Gary

Cooper. Coincidentally, we were also related to Gary Cooper. "I'm not sure exactly how," my father said. "But it's on your grandmother's side. One of her uncles married a Cooper."

On our visits to Valier, my father and cousins would sit underneath the maple trees and speculate, spinning out a thin string of conversation, like a spider building a web, attaching our family to some well-known personality. One evening, my cousin Clarence mentioned *The Sonny and Cher Comedy Hour*, then playing on Wednesday nights.

"We're related to her, you know," my father said.

"Related to who?" I asked.

"Cher," Dad said. "She was a Mackey on your grandmother's side."

My grandmother Mackey's family was so large they could have formed their own country. Invariably, every famous person we were related to was on the Mackey side of our family tree.

Clarence frowned. "I thought Cher was a Cherokee."

"Yep, that's right," Dad said. "She's one of the Cherokee Mackeys."

"How come I never heard of this until now?" Clarence asked.

"Beats me," Dad said. "She used to come to the family reunions when she was a kid. Tall, skinny kid. Long black hair."

"I didn't know she was a Mackey," Pooner said. "Is that her last name? Cher Mackey?"

"Must be," my father said, clearly relieved no one present seemed to know Cher's last name.

When I returned to school in the fall, I told all my friends I was related to Cher. Since none of them knew her last name, it was an easy sell, and my standing among my peers rose. Being related to Cher turned out to be the highlight of my younger years, and I spoke about our kinship eagerly and often to anyone who would listen. I also told them about my humble origins, descended as I was from Belgian glass-workers and miners of coal, just to let them know I was as common as the next man, a regular Joe, who although related to famous people, never let it go to my head.

Chapter 8

Miss Huddleston

When I was in the sixth grade, I nearly died. Nearly dying is vastly superior to dying. It is every bit as dramatic, but not as permanent. My parents took me to several doctors, none of whom were able to diagnose my illness. I was tired all the time, irritable, and perspired constantly. My mother had been suffering the same symptoms, and for a while I thought I was menopausal, but that turned out not to be the case.

Peanut was a great fan of *Ripley's Believe It or Not!* and enjoyed nothing more than working an odd fact into conversation whenever he could. "Maybe you have the plague," he said, then pointed out, rather cheerfully, that it had killed seventy-five million people in the Middle Ages. "All it takes is one flea bite and you're a goner. I read about it in *Ripley's Believe It or Not!*"

Fleas, we had. Our dog Zipper was thick with them and had scratched her fur off down to the pink, with the exception of a few tufts of fur she couldn't reach. She looked like a victim of radiation poisoning.

I spent three weeks on the living room couch, eating cherry popsicles and watching reruns of *Petticoat Junction.* Peanut had told me that in the opening credits of the show, when Bobbie Jo, Billie Jo, and Betty Jo were swimming in the water tank, you could see them naked if you looked closely. I'd never seen a naked woman before, though not for lack of trying. Like generations of youth before me, I scoured each issue of the *National Geographic* in our school library, hoping to glimpse an uncovered breast. Mrs. McNeff, the school librarian, was diligent about removing such pictures from the *Geographic,* but had missed one and Billy Grubb had found it. Billy Grubb had a nose for depravity and was voted Most Likely to Become a Pervert our senior year of high school.

All I ever saw of Bobbie Jo, Billie Jo, and Betty Jo were their necks and a hint of collarbone, and even that was fuzzy. We lived thirty miles from the television tower and *Petticoat Junction* came in blurry, even when I wrapped tin foil around the antenna. Even so, I became enchanted with the madcap antics of Eb Dawson, Newt Kiley, and Floyd Smoot, and was hooked on the show by the end of the first week.

It was a splendid three weeks, my poor health notwithstanding. My brother Doug told my teacher, Miss Huddleston, I was dying, so she never bothered sending home any homework. Instead, she had the class make an It's-Been-Nice-Knowing-You card, and had everyone at school sign it, even Roydeena Feltner, who wrote that she was sorry for hitting me and that I was the bravest person she'd ever met.

Eventually, my mother took me to Dr. Kirtley, who tested me for mononucleosis.

"They call it the kissing disease, you know," Dr. Kirtley said. "Somebody been kissing you?" He winked at my mother.

I had two aunts—big-lipped women who wore bright orange lipstick and stuck their lips to my cheeks like suction cups. Whenever they were within arm's length, they'd pull me to them and glom on to my cheek like a sucker fish. Now it appeared they had infected me. Killed by my big-lipped aunts.

Fortunately, the test for mono came back negative. Dr. Kirtley ran more tests, which came up empty, so my parents began losing interest and gave me up for dead. I was the runt of the litter anyway and the prospects for my survival had always been dim. Child mortality rates were higher then, and people had extra kids to make up for the ones they lost. As concern for my well-being waned, I sensed I was on my own health-wise; my resolve deepened, and I began to recover. But for three weeks, the buzzards were circling.

The worst part of missing school was being away from Miss Huddleston, who looked a lot like Betty Jo. Every teacher I'd ever had was a hundred years old, with large flaps of fat underneath their upper arms that jiggled when they wrote on the chalkboard. But Miss Huddleston was lovely beyond compare—proof of God's creative benevolence.

That year someone in the school office decreed that we should be taught sex education and assigned another lovely young teacher, whose name now eludes me, to instruct us. Truancy among the boys plummeted to record lows. Kent Fender, never a diligent scholar, began skipping lunch to arrive early at sex education for a front-row seat. We took careful notes, asked probing questions, and urged our teacher to draw illustrations on the chalkboard.

Thoroughly galvanized by the curriculum, Kent Fender ordered a pair of x-ray glasses from the back of a comic book ("See through walls! See through clothes! Surprise and amaze your friends!") and brought them to school for further research. Unfortunately, he was careless in their use, and slipped them on just as Mrs. Stanley—all four hundred pounds, not including her beard—walked into our classroom and into his x-ray vision. Kent let out a shriek, fainted dead away, and the glasses were broken in the fall.

Of course, some of my peers would urge our teacher to delve into the more curious aspects of human sexuality.

"Tell us about hermaphrodites," Suds Norton said when the teacher was explaining the differences between men and women. He turned to Kent Fender. "There's some people, they're born with a winkie and an angina. The doctors just lop off the winkie, but sometimes they get it wrong, so you end up with a man who's winkieless."

Suds Norton was an expert on sexuality, having glanced through a *Playboy* magazine behind the counter at the Rexall drugstore. Suds had voyeurism down to a fine art. He would give Peanut a quarter to distract the pharmacist with a conversation about various poxes and diseases, then duck behind the counter, peruse the magazine, sketching the more salient features, which he showed to our teacher and got sent to the principal's office.

As attractive as our sex education teacher was, I still believed Miss Huddleston was vastly superior. To my great delight, Miss Huddleston seemed genuinely fond of me. She would pause from her instruction to pat me on the head, calling me her little monkey. I did all I could to encourage her affection, staying after school to wash the chalkboard, clap the erasers, and empty the pencil sharpener. I had been an indifferent student, but wanting desperately to please her, my grades soared.

"I sure will miss you next year," she said one late winter day, patting me on the head.

The realization hit me like a thunderbolt. In trying to impress her, I had wrecked my chances of getting to repeat sixth grade with Miss Huddleston. The seventh grade was in another building across town. I wouldn't even be able to glimpse her in the hallway. Faced with this sorry predicament, my only option was to get in so much trouble I would be held back.

My opportunity came the very next day, when I brought a magnifying glass to school and used it to concentrate the sun's rays onto the vinyl roof of Mr. Leavitt's car during recess. I waited until Mrs. Stanley was watching, lest my delinquency go unnoticed.

A thin curl of blue smoke rose from the roof. Mrs. Stanley began waddling toward me, her face darkening.

"What do you think you're doing?" she asked.

"Burning a hole in Mr. Leavitt's car," I answered helpfully.

"We'll see about that," she said, seizing me by the ear, twisting and cracking the cartilage, then goose-stepped me to Principal Peter's office, where she deposited me in the straight-back chair across from his desk and, quivering with indignation, said, "You'll never believe what I caught this young man doing."

He peered at me over the top of his glasses, not saying anything for a long moment. "What do you have to say for yourself?" he asked, finally.

Principals and teachers always asked that question whenever a kid got in trouble, leading us to believe if we supplied a reasonable explanation we might go free. It never worked. It was simply the cat toying with the mouse before devouring it.

I hung my head. "I don't deserve to pass," I told him. "You should hold me back a year."

Instead, I got three whacks, hard, with the paddle, and had to tell Mr. Leavitt what I'd done and pay for the duct tape to patch the vinyl roof. Plus, I was made to stay after school for a month and clean all the chalkboards, which caused my lungs to fill with chalk dust and for the next several weeks, whenever I coughed, I expelled a fine, white powder. I bore that hardship with good cheer, Miss Huddleston being worth the suffering.

I would sit in class, writing her name next to my mine, then drawing a heart around us. It took some sleuthing to learn her first name. In those days, all my teachers had one of three first names—Miss, Mrs., or Mr. But I overheard another teacher call her Rebecca, and armed with this delicious little intimacy, I imagined we were married and wrote her name in long rows up and down my notebook paper.

Mrs. Rebecca Gulley
Mrs. Rebecca Gulley
Mrs. Rebecca Gulley
Mrs. Rebecca Gulley
Mrs. Rebecca Gulley
Mrs. Rebecca Gulley

But mine was a love that dared not speak its name, students and teachers being natural enemies, adversaries since time immemorial. To cross this boundary was a serious breach of protocol, a violation of God's plan, but Miss Huddleston was so enchanting I could not help myself.

My inappropriate longings would have remained a secret, had Tim Hadley not seen my doodles. He cornered me on the playground one Friday afternoon.

"You're in love with Miss Huddleston, aren't you?" he asked.

I hesitated, a dead giveaway.

He punched me on the shoulder. "You goober. You're not supposed to love a teacher. That's sick."

"I can't help myself," I said, my sense of shame rising.

"You just need a little education, that's all," Tim said. "Sit behind me tonight at the movie," he said. "Don't say anything. Just watch."

I met him that night at the Royal Theater, and after buying my popcorn took a seat behind Tim and his current flame, a girl named Leah. The movie, *Battle for the Planet of the Apes*, was about a gorilla inciting a civil war among the apes. It was in the romance/monkey documentary/war genre. "Guaranteed," Tim told me, "to drive a girl into the arms of the nearest available man."

I paid little attention to the movie, instead studying Tim's technique, which was so casual as to appear almost indifferent. He chomped happily on his popcorn, pausing every now and then to comment on an ape and take a slurp of soda, scarcely paying any attention to Leah. This was entirely consistent with the prevailing theory of conquest—that appearing uninterested in a girl was the quickest way to secure her affection.

I imagined Miss Huddleston was seated beside me, us smooching with our popcorn-buttered lips, snuggling closer when the gorilla General Aldo, brilliantly portrayed by Claude Akins, tried to incite a simian civil war. In my fantasy I pulled Miss Huddleston to me, calming her, patting her flab-free upper arm until she was soothed.

Tim walked Leah home after the movie. I followed behind at a discreet distance, imagining Miss Huddleston's thin, delicate fingers interlaced with mine. By now, we were on a first-name basis and I was calling her Becky. Matters didn't seem to be going as well for Tim; his prospects for romance were fading. When they arrived at Leah's house, she mumbled a quick good-bye and ducked inside, without even a handshake.

"There's your first lesson," Tim said. "Don't ever take a girl to a monkey movie."

While that night was a bust girl-wise, it began our fascination with simians, which culminated in my spending every Friday night at Tim's home, watching *Planet of the Apes* on television and eating Pringles potato chips, falling asleep in the blue glow of late-night television, waking up in the morning to Pringle crumbs scattered on the floor around us, our teeth sticky-brown with Coke.

Tim lived on a farm south of town. When school ended on Friday and I'd delivered my papers, I'd ride my bike to his house, carrying my toothbrush and a change of clothing in my bug backpack. It was a perilous journey, past Joe Johnson's farmhouse and his pack of attack dogs. Johnson's house was halfway up a long hill. By the time I pulled even with their driveway and entered the dogs' killing zone, I was worn out. The dogs were waiting, their fur matted with blood from disemboweling the last child to ride past. They would swarm over me, pull me off the bike, and shred my various appendages until Joe Johnson would stick his head out the front door and call them off. I would push my bicycle the rest of the way up the hill, then coast down the opposite side all the way to Tim's house, leaving a blood trail, like a wounded animal.

Nowadays, a dog attack would make the front page of the newspaper, the owner would be arrested, and the dog euthanized. But back then dog attacks were routine occurrences, part and parcel of the childhood experience. Dogs roamed freely about, copulating at will, terrorizing small children, and strewing garbage up and down the streets. When I showed my father my wounds, how my right arm was connected by the merest sliver of flesh, he said, "Yep, that's a dog bite all right," then went back to reading the *Great Hoosier Daily.*

All in all, my sixth grade year was a perilous time, what with plagues and dogs threatening me at every turn. I probably wouldn't have survived, but I didn't want to die without first kissing a girl, so I persisted, against the odds, my fantasies of Miss Huddleston a warm comfort against the chill of celibacy.

Chapter 9

Carnival

To be a child in those years was to live for the summers, freed from the manacles of education and its attendant miseries. Summers were a bacchanalian feast, one day after another of unrestrained liberty—camping overnight in Doc Gibb's apple orchard, riding our bikes on the back roads to the next town, floating down White Lick Creek on inner tubes.

Our town's descent into decadence reached its zenith the first week of July, when the Poor Jack Carnival landed in our town. On Wednesday evening, Merle Funk, the chief of police, would rope off the square to traffic. Later that night, well after dark, a convoy of trucks and trailers would roll in from the east on U.S. 36. Peanut and I would sit on our bicycles in front of the Dairy Queen, listening for the strain of their engines as they climbed the hill in front of the Laundromat.

They would lurch into view near the junior high school—a string of trucks covered in dust and grime from exotic locales. Dirt with a story behind it. The drivers, we knew for a fact, were escaped criminals, convicts on the lam, hiding out in the carnival. The week before the carnival came, Merle Funk wrote a letter to the local newspaper advising caution while the carnies were in town. "Chief of Police Anticipates Crime Wave," the headline in the *Republican* read. We locked our doors and hid our valuables. The Minkners, Catholic to the core, would move their Blessed Virgin Mary from the flowerbed in their front yard to their garage, cover Christ's mother with a tarp, and pile lawn furniture on top of her.

"The carnies will steal you blind," Mr. Minkner told me. "Steal the shingles from your roof, if they weren't nailed down."

Smilcy and Emmalyne Dinsmore owned Dinsmore's, the basket shop on the town square, and would display wicker furniture and baskets on the sidewalk during the summer. When the carnival came to town, their son Earl stood guard over the merchandise. Earl was a huge block of a man and would have looked menacing, except that he smiled constantly, his big white teeth shining like a flashlight.

Dinsmore's had once been a grocery store, but when Kroger hit town, they switched to baskets. In the rear of the store were remnants of their grocery days—dusty canned goods, petrified chunks of meat, and a staggering number of hairnets. Hundreds of hairnets, as if a hairnet convention had come to town and Smiley had over-anticipated the demand. Emmalyne would wear them, hoping to launch a fad and clear their shelves, but the trend never took hold, not even among the carnies, whose hair fell into the cotton candy machine and was twirled up into a pink Pentecostal hairdo, served on a stick, then washed down with a lemon shake-up.

While Peanut and I were waiting at the Dairy Queen, watching for the carnival trucks to roll into town, he would regale me with stories of carnivals past, the near misses and tragedies of carnie life. "There was this one guy I heard about who worked for a carnival, and he got his hair caught in one of the rides, and it ripped his scalp clean off. I saw a picture of him in *Ripley's Believe It or Not.* They did a skin transplant on him, but they took the skin from his butt and when his hair grew back out, it was all fuzzy."

This jibed with the prevailing theory of carnie workers, who seemed, among all the professionals I encountered, to be uniquely visited by the weirdest, worst luck. I was captivated by the carnies, but terrified of them at the same time, and half expected them to reach across the counter, grab me by the throat, and kill me. I was especially intrigued by their indifference and studied boredom, scooping up quarters and dropping them into their aprons, carelessly sliding the .22 rifle across the counter so I could knock down three ducks and win a bullwhip. Two ducks down, but never the third. I always had to settle for a plastic troll with long wild hair, in sore need of a hairnet.

By the end of carnival week, Peanut and I had collected dozens of trolls, which we pretended were carnies, their hair caught in our bicycle chains, their squat fat bodies pulverized by the sprockets. "First thing I'd do if I were a carnie," Peanut said, "is shave my head."

When I was twelve I toyed with the notion of becoming a carnie, of drifting from town to town, never bathing, letting my hair grow long, getting a tattoo, and learning to blow smoke rings. Writing home every now and then to ease my parents' minds, who were opposed to my being in the carnival, but would change their tune once I married the Wild Girl of Borneo and gave them carnie grandchildren to fuss over.

With an eye toward making the carnival our careers, Peanut and I persuaded the carnies to let us test the rides. No pay, but all the hairy cotton candy we could eat. The carnies would assemble the rides through the night—the Tilt-A-Whirl, Ferris wheel, Scrambler, and my personal favorite, the Rocket Ship. Peanut and I would show up first thing in the morning, when they needed test dummies.

"I don't know about this," Peanut said. "One time, over in Amo, they put this big, fat kid in the Rocket Ship, the bolts snapped, and down he went. Corkscrewed into the asphalt going two hundred. Had to scrape him off the pavement. Wasn't enough left to put in a casket."

Our probable deaths only added to the thrill.

The entire town square was closed for the carnival, and the business owners hated it. The smart ones closed down and went on vacation for a week, leaving Merle Funk to guard their stores. The others bellyached, wrote letters to the editor, had heart attacks, and died early from the stress.

The Scrambler was set up outside Otis Marlow's law office. His desk sat near the front window. The cars on the Scrambler would hurtle toward him like a buzz bomb, veering away at the last second. He spent the week flinching, took up drink, and died from a pickled liver twenty years later. Killed by the carnival, just like the fat boy from Amo, but with less of a splat.

The churches were not of one mind regarding the carnival. The Catholics were generally supportive, tolerating debauchery so long as those committing it didn't use birth control, but the Baptists and Pentecostals were sorely opposed to the carnival. Their pastors began preaching against it the month before it steamed into port, their ire building each week. Verses from the books of Leviticus and Revelation were cited—warnings against making merry when the return of the Lord was at hand. The Quakers were silent on the matter, but suspected carnival attendance bordered on sin and were embarrassed when they saw one another there, justifying their presence by praying for those attending, that they would come to the Lord while there was time. Like most young people, I considered myself invincible and planned on coming to the Lord later, when I was old and dried up and had had my fun.

The churches were united on the you-never-know policy, that life was uncertain. If the fat boy in Amo had come along five minutes later, some other kid would have landed on the asphalt. If Otis Marlow had rented a law office a week earlier, he could have gotten the one next to the Baker Hardware store, where they set up the Ferris wheel, which would have been considerably better for his nerves, and he wouldn't have taken up drink and wrecked his life. He would have joined the Jaycees, won the John Jenner Outstanding Citizen Award, and retired to Florida. Instead, he ended up at the Buckhorn Bar, deep in the cups. Timing is everything.

If my timing had been better, I might have hit that third duck and won a bullwhip, instead of a troll. But Donny Shaw, a fourteen-year-old with a rap sheet running six pages, saw me carrying a troll, called me a pansy, and beat me up, which shot my reputation. There are people who still talk about it behind my back and snicker when they see me. Donny Shaw joined the carnival and left town, which surprised no one. Some people are born to the carnie life; others have it thrust upon them. Donny was born for it. He came out of his mother's womb tattooed and smoking a Marlboro. When he moved away, the town laid off three policeman.

Peanut and I didn't let trifling matters such as theft, assault, and death by Rocket Ship dampen our enthusiasm. July was our high-water mark, carnival wise. The Poor Jack Carnival on the town square was followed by the 4-H carnival, set up in the vacant field next to the county jail, which made it convenient for the carnies who'd been arrested. In the pokey one minute, bailed out and running the Scrambler the next.

The 4-H carnival was a rat-trap outfit, the rides rusted and jerry-rigged, bandaged with duct tape at critical joints. No parents with half a brain allowed their children anywhere near the place.

"It's a death wish," my mother said. "I wouldn't let my dog on those rides."*

Each summer, the 4-H carnival sported a different name to fend off creditors, new logos painted on top of old ones, but always the same operators—black-toothed, cigarette-skinny men at the end of the carnival road. They were not the kind of people to whom one could comfortably entrust their child's safety. My mother could sense danger in the next state over—she had a nose for it—and detested the carnival to no end.

"Any mother who would let her children on those rides must not love them," she told me.

But by the last night of the carnival, I had worn her down with my incessant pleading.

"Go ahead," my mother would yell, after I'd asked her for the umpteenth time, "but if you end up crippled for life, don't say I didn't warn you."

Don't say I didn't warn you! was my mother's mantra, her parental aria, sung at every occasion that could even remotely end in my death or dismemberment, including running with scissors, riding a bicycle, or playing Little League baseball. Like Peanut, she knew of hundreds of children

* We had two dogs, Zipper and Fanny, both of whom frequented the carnival and hung out near the trash cans, hoping to snag a half-eaten elephant ear. Fanny was a harlot and popped out puppies nine weeks after every carnival she ever attended.

who'd been spectacularly maimed while pursuing the activities I wished to undertake. She was not only death on carnivals, repeating Peanut's Amo fat-boy narrative, she added to it with gruesome tales of severed limbs, crushed heads, and boys, just like me, accidentally castrated by flying machine parts. *Don't say I didn't warn you!*

My mother descended into a catatonic state the week before the 4-H fair, certain it would be my last week on earth, that if the carnival rides didn't do me in, the livestock would—a rampaging bull, a mule kick to the head, a crazed chicken pecking my eyes out. Blindness by chicken had happened to the neighbor of a friend's cousin, or so my mother claimed. The child had entered the poultry tent and was mugged by a Rhode Island Red, out of its chicken mind on growth steroids. The child was pecked blind before adults could pull the chicken off. The prospect of witnessing such carnage only increased my determination to attend the county fair.

In terms of pure excitement, the Exhibition Hall ran a close second to the carnival rides. Four long rows of local businesses and organizations passing out free merchandise—refrigerator magnets, helium balloons, cups of water (which we peed out later behind the horse barn), ballpoint pens, pencils, paper fans from Baker's Funeral Home (*Providing for You and Yours Since 1923!*), plastic badges from the sheriff's department, and my personal favorite—signing up to receive a home visit from the minister of the Church of Christ. Peanut and I filled out Church of Christ cards by the hour, stuffing their box with our entries, each one bearing the name of someone we didn't like.

The Church of Christ folk were persistent. They met resistance with girded loins, interpreting opposition as Satan's handiwork, fueling their efforts to evangelize the reluctant. "No, thank you" and "I'm not interested" only stirred them to action. They loved the carnival for its evangelical possibilities, lying in wait for the swarms of sinners it attracted. The Church of Christers were thick about the place, men in white shirts and black pants passing out tracts that described in colorful detail the ultimate destination of the spiritually suspect. I loved reading their literature, which contained vivid illustrations of Catholics and other heretics roasting in the flames. Ecumenism fell low on their list of priorities.

I'm not sure what would have distressed my mother more—my running off with the carnival or joining the Church of Christ. A staunch Catholic, she was generally alarmed by Protestantism. Years later, when I told her I wanted to be a Quaker pastor, she tried talking me out of it, urging me toward the law. It is startling now to realize my mother considered a career as a lawyer to be more virtuous than ministry.

The carnival no longer comes to Danville. The interests of business eventually overrode the interests of fun, and Poor Jack was sent packing. The blame was placed on the inability of firefighters to reach a potential blaze on the town square with the carnival rides in the way, but I suspect it became impractical to shut down the town square businesses for a week when there was money to be made. It was not unlike the loss of our Sabbath rest, our one week each year to spin circles in the sky, seated on the Ferris wheel, rising high above the earth, the stars shimmering overhead, just waiting to be grabbed.

Chapter 10

My Dalliance With Religion

We attended church at St. Mary's Catholic Church, on the west edge of town, across from Johnston's IGA, next to Pleas Lilly's gas station. Father McLaughlin was our priest, a kind but tedious man who was easily scandalized. On Saturday afternoons, I would stand in line, waiting my turn in the confessional, the silence punctuated by occasional outbursts from Father's booth—"You did what? . . . With whom? . . . Oh, for Pete's sake!"

No matter what anyone did, the penance was always the same—three Hail Marys and two Our Fathers. As far as the Church was concerned, murdering your parents required no more contrition than violating any of the obscure tenets of the Roman Catholic Church.

"Forgive me, Father, for I have sinned. It has been seven days since my last confession. Since then, I ate a hamburger on Friday, then killed my parents and buried them in the basement."

"You ate meat on Friday? For Pete's sake! That'll be three Hail Marys and two Our Fathers."

This verified what my Protestant friends said, that Catholics were weak on sin. In my mind, this was a selling point of Catholicism and one we Catholics should have used to our advantage. Sinning in the Protestant church got you sent to hell, while sinning in the Catholic church got you sent to purgatory, which wasn't torture, but neither was it enjoyable, kind of like flying coach. But just as soon as your loved ones lit a candle for you, the priest would say a prayer and you were upgraded to first class. So far as I could tell, Catholicism was the better deal.

One of my earliest memories of being Catholic was my first communion. I suspected it was a big deal because my grandmother rode the Greyhound bus up from Vincennes and my mom bought me a new white shirt from Beecham's Menswear on the square. Father McLaughlin prayed over a plate of thin, pale wafers, then said they'd been turned into the body of Christ, but I had my doubts. Mr. Bolton lived down the street from us and dabbled in magic. He could turn a handkerchief into a flower, and it looked like a flower.

Father McLaughlin wasn't nearly as adept at magic. His wafers looked nothing like Jesus.

First communion was followed by several years of intense instruction—Sister Mary John demonstrating, by the clever use of flannelgraphs, how Roman Catholicism was the One True Church. This culminated in my confirmation at the age of thirteen, when the bishop drove out from the city in a Cadillac and laid his hands on me. Among the Catholic clergy, car ownership hinged on one's status. Or so my brother Glenn told me. The Pope, he said, drove a Mercedes, the bishops drove Cadillacs. Father McLaughlin drove a Ford Pinto.

According to Sister Mary John, I was supposed to feel the presence of the Holy Spirit, but I felt the same way I always felt in church—a cluelessness tinged with a vague fear. Sister Mary John had shown us a flannelgraph of the apostles receiving the Holy Spirit on the day of Pentecost. They looked quite happy, except that their hair was on fire. Confirmation, the sister explained, was the pinnacle of our spiritual lives, when the power of the Holy Spirit would come upon us. But I was suspicious of a religion whose high point was the igniting of one's head, and my enthusiasm for church, which had never been great, began to fade.

Being burnt to a turn for the sake of Jesus seemed consistent with everything I knew about the Catholics, who seemed captivated by the idea of suffering for one's faith. Lining the sanctuary were the Stations of the Cross, a travelogue of sorts, fourteen pictures of Jesus getting seriously whupped on by the Romans. I would study them during Mass, wondering what Jesus had done to make the Italians so mad.

Jesus, according to Sister Mary John, was the first Catholic, and thereby suffered for his faith, just as we, his servants, endure persecution. Our town had an abundance of Puritans, whose sole ambition was to rescue us from the clutches of the Pope and deliver us to the safe waters of Protestantism. We were a pathetic band of believers and seemed to invite harassment, as if God had taped a *Kick Me* sign to our backs.

Chick was the first in our family to leave the One True Church. When she turned seventeen, in a fit of teenage rebellion, she joined with the Baptists, who promptly dunked her, her Catholic baptism being not only insufficient, but heretical. My mother was appalled, but I was secretly delighted, privately urging my sister to expand the parameters of religious liberty so I could one day escape the clutches of organized religion myself.

The Sunday morning of my sister's second baptism, my mother went to the Catholic church to pray for her, while my father and I accompanied Chick to the Baptist church to watch. The church was packed, deliverance from Catholicism being rare. Before plunging my sister beneath the waters, the pastor announced that Jeanne (for a moment, I wondered who he was talking about since we'd always called my sister Chick) had grown up in the Catholic Church, but had decided to become a Christian, to which the great throng responded with "Amen!" and "Praise the Lord!" I had been under the impression Catholics were Christian, but found myself swept along with the tide and thought of getting dunked myself, just in case the Baptists were right.

The pastor pushed my sister under until her legs began to kick, then raised her up to a new, albeit damp, life, handed her a pink bath towel, and had everyone come forward to shake her hand and congratulate her for being saved. We went downstairs and sealed her fate over meat loaf, green beans, and sweet iced tea—delicious food that helped my father and me feel more charitable toward the Baptists.

The Baptist church was strategically located across the street from the jail. The Baptists' stained glass window showed Jesus extending his hand toward the inmates. The prisoners were welcome in the Baptist church, and any of the town's other churches, so long as they cleaned up their act, got a haircut, found a job, served on a committee, and voted Republican.

While there were theological differences among the churches in our town, we were of one mind when it came to politics. God was a Republican, the Democrats being soft on communism. The Sunday Father McLaughlin read from the second chapter of Acts how the early church "sold their possessions and goods and distributed the proceeds to all, as any had need," he skated perilously close to communism. Mr. Vaughn rose to his feet, walked out, and joined the Baptists.

This branded Father McLaughlin as a radical, which was confirmed when he booted Mrs. Gregg off the organ and replaced her with a guitarist. The next week he was seen at

Johnston's IGA wearing blue jeans, and his fate was sealed. He was gone the next month, transferred to the city to live with the Democrats. A Father Coffin, who was 110 years old and aptly named, took his place.

Since I had been visited by the Holy Spirit at my confirmation, I was eligible to serve as an altar boy, which involved my wearing a long black dress and holding a golden plate underneath the chin of whomever was receiving communion in the event Father Coffin accidentally dropped Jesus' body. The plate had a wooden handle and a sharp edge, which could be used to chop unsuspecting communicants in the Adam's apple just as Father was placing the wafer on their tongues. It paid to stay on the good side of altar boys.

The Adam's apple, Sister Mary John told us, was God's way of reminding us we'd been born into sin, glaring proof of Adam's disobedience. We boys looked in the mirror and there it was—a chunk of forbidden fruit stuck in our throats, compliments of our ancestors, who'd had a good gig going, lounging around buck naked in a beautiful garden, then had blown it all to hell, and we were still paying for it, all these years later.

Original sin wasn't even original when you thought about it. I would sit in church and imagine much more innovative ways Adam could have sinned. He was in a garden with a naked woman, for crying out loud. What guy in his right mind would have taken time to talk with a snake and eat an apple? What a doofus Adam was.

All the churches in our town, in addition to the Republican question, were in accord on the matter of original sin. We were born into sin, doomed to hell from the start, our very presence an affront to God, according to Sister Mary John. Larry Lawson had the largest Adam's apple in town, a telltale sign of his sinful nature. He drank, cussed, and cheated on his wife. Mildred Havens volunteered at the hospital, fed stray animals, and gave most of her money to orphans. But both Larry and Mildred were headed to hell in a handbasket, and there was nothing they could do about it except throw themselves on the mercy of God. It made no sense to me, but Sister Mary John said the ways of the Lord were mysterious and not to be questioned.

Still, I had many questions. I wondered why women couldn't be priests. So far as I could tell, the main difference between men and women was the plumbing. Why did being a priest require a winkie? And let's say I died while saving someone's life on my way to confession. Would God still send me to hell for having unconfessed sin, or would I get credit for saving a life? I asked Sister Mary John, but she wasn't sure. That was another question I had. Why was a woman named John?

My biggest question about church was why I had to go. When I asked my mother, she said, "Because I said so, that's why."

Because I said so was her reason for why I should do everything I didn't want to do, every time I didn't want to do it.

What I mostly didn't want to do was go to church, which I found excruciating. I wasn't even sure I believed in God, my ardent prayers for a girlfriend having gone unanswered. If there was a God, he was indifferent about my love life. I spoke about it with Peanut, who told me each denomination had its own god and that I'd had the bad luck of belonging to a church whose god didn't care for sex. The priests couldn't have it, the nuns couldn't have it, and the rest of us could only have it when we wanted children, otherwise we had to confine our affections to a brief handshake.*

For a religion opposed to sex, we Catholics seemed taken with it. We had a large cross behind the altar, from which Jesus hung in his skivvies. At first, I thought this was a peculiarity of St. Mary's, but Jesus was dressed that way in every Catholic church I ever attended. It didn't stop there. The little old Catholic ladies carried pictures in their purses of Jesus darn near naked, and even wore him on prayer beads around their necks. When I had my confirmation, the priest gave me a rosary from which an undressed Jesus dangled. I hid it under my mattress so my friends wouldn't see it and think I played on the pink team.

Believing suffering drew us closer to God, the Catholics made worship as miserable as possible. Our church had no air-conditioning, and the windows didn't open. Each Sunday in the summer, we'd lose several congregants to heat exhaustion. They would collapse, their heads thumping the floor like watermelons. The ushers would hurry forward, grab the wretched souls by their ankles, and drag them

* Eventually, I earned a graduate degree in theology and learned there was only one God, who was utterly opposed to sex, unless the people having it were married and didn't enjoy themselves.

from the sanctuary. Father Coffin never missed a beat, forging ahead with Mass.

According to Sister Mary John, persistence in the face of difficulty was the chief difference between Protestants and Catholics. We were willing to endure hardship for the sake of Jesus, while Protestants basked in air-conditioning listening to their ministers prattle on about God's love. "They're cool now, but it's going to be hot for them later," she said, showing us Methodists roasting on flannelgraph flames.

Sister Mary John was well versed on the finer points of Catholic theology, addressing a range of topics ranging from dietary laws—no meat on Fridays, but you could drink all the beer you wanted—to the proper hand placement while praying. "Your hands," she said, "should be placed together, palm to palm, your fingertips pointing toward God in heaven. Do not pray with your fingers pointing downward, lest you inadvertently pray to Satan."

Praying to Beelzebub! This filled me with alarm. I worried I had accidentally prayed to Ol' Scratch. From what Sister Mary John had told us about the devil, it was just like him to trick us into praying to him. He was sneaky that way. Religious life was a precarious one, not unlike a minefield, one misstep from obliteration. One minute we were saying Hail Marys and eating the body of Christ, the next moment we were praying to the Prince of Darkness, headed straight to hell on greased skids.

While we were opposed to Satan, we did admire his work ethic. He labored around the clock, leading us astray with card playing, dancing, movie going, miniskirts, rock and roll, sex education, birth control, and wealth. Of those temptations, we knew wealth to be the most pernicious. "It is easier for a camel to go through the eye of a needle than for a rich man to enter the Kingdom of God," Jesus told the rich young ruler. The rich young rulers attended the Episcopal church on Washington Street, where they were soft on sin.

Sitting in the Catholic church on Sunday mornings, scrunched between my brothers Glenn and David, their bony elbows digging into my sides, the pew hard against my backbone, Glenn surreptitiously wetting his finger and sticking it in my ear, I would study the Stations of the Cross, thanking Jesus for suffering so I could go to heaven and live with my family forever, except for my sister, who'd left the One True Church and was at that moment sitting on a padded pew, her ears being tickled by the soft gospel of Protestantism. Father Coffin would drone on in Latin, his gentle cadence interrupted by the sound of heads striking the floor with a hollow wallop, which was, in those Catholic years, the sound of faith to me.

Chapter 11

Halloween

Of all the holidays, Halloween was my favorite, topping even Christmas, where some sort of reciprocity was expected. Halloween was a one-way street, all of its riches headed my way. I wasn't sure when Halloween had been invented, but knew it had to have been dreamed up by a kid. No adult in his or her right mind would ever have said, "Let's have kids go door-to-door, and we'll give them candy, and if we don't, they can soap our windows and throw toilet paper in our trees. It'll be fun."

My early Halloweens were perilous affairs. I dressed as a ghost, a bedsheet draped over me. We were too poor to waste a sheet, so my mother never cut holes for my eyes. My brother Glenn was supposed to hold my hand and guide me from house to house, but as soon as we turned the corner and were out of my parents' eyesight, he would launch out on his own and leave me to my own devices. I would stumble from house to house, tripping over curbs, running into cars, smacking headlong into trees, and spilling my candy. The other children would swarm over me, like hyenas on a downed gazelle, fighting over my Tootsie Rolls and Smarties.

Nevertheless, I enjoyed the idea of Halloween and sensed its potential. Within a few years I had ditched the sheet, dressed as a bum wearing my grandfather's old clothes, and with all my faculties restored was making out like a bandit.

At the age of thirteen I believed I had reached my Halloween zenith, but hadn't counted on Peanut and his near-genius capacity for candy collection.

"You're small potatoes," he told me a few weeks before Halloween. "You get dressed up as a bum, which is fine, but you only go one night. Me, I trick-or-treat five nights. Two nights before, the night of, and two nights after."

I stared at him, stunned.

"I get enough candy at Halloween to last all the way to Easter," he said. "I get enough candy at Easter to last me through to Halloween. I never spend money on candy."

It was true. By then I had known Peanut three years and had never seen him buy even the smallest piece of candy.

As stunning as that achievement was, he would surpass even his wildest aspirations in 1974, when he and I, after weeks of careful planning, collected candy from every house in Danville, except the Bryants' who were Jehovah's Witnesses and didn't celebrate Halloween.

I wish I could claim credit for this thunderbolt inspiration, but it was Peanut's idea, and his alone.

We'd ridden our bicycles to Baker's Hardware to look at the Miss Hardware calendar, our usual Saturday morning pursuit, when Peanut spied a new map of Danville hanging on the wall above Rawleigh Baker's desk.

"Got some more if you want one," Rawleigh Baker said. "Just had some printed up. Here, give one to your folks." He handed us each a town map.

We rode home and studied the maps on my front porch, marking the points of interest—Denise Turner's house, the Dairy Queen, the house of the lady on Mulberry Street who walked around naked and didn't close her blinds.

Peanut peered at the map. "You know," he said. "I never noticed this before, but if a fella wanted to, he could divide this town into pieces."

He pulled a stubby pencil from his shirt pocket and with several strokes quickly divided the town into five equal sections.

"So what," I said.

"And if we rode our bikes instead of walked, I bet we could hit every house in a section in one night. Do that five nights in a row, and we could trick-or-treat at every house in Danville."

It was an idea startling in its audacity.

My father served on the town board. We asked him how many houses there were in Danville.

“A dab under one thousand,” he said, without hesitation.

Whether it involved bug spray or civic affairs, my father was a numbers man without peer.

The trick-or-treating protocol permitted a three hour window of solicitation, from six to nine PM. Peanut did the math is his head. “One thousand homes divided by five equals two hundred homes, divided by one-hundred-and-eighty minutes equals a little over one minute per house.

“Can't use paper bags,” he continued. “They'll bust. Too much candy. We'll have to use burlap bags.”

It worked precisely as Peanut had predicted. A few citizens grumbled on the first and fifth days, muttering at us about trick-or-treating outside the proper Halloween parameters, but most of them forked over candy just the same.

“That's the only bad thing about it,” Peanut said. “If somebody doesn't give us candy, we don't have time to soap their windows.”

As well as it worked, our enterprise was not without its setbacks. I'd worn a hobo mask, a gross miscalculation, resulting in homeowner after homeowner trying to guess my identity, which threw off our schedule. “Who is that under there? Petie York? James Martin? Is that you, James? Mildred, come here and see if you can tell who this is.”

“It's me, Phil Gulley. Norm and Gloria's boy,” I'd say, hoping to hurry them along.

“That can't be. Why, the last time I saw you, you were knee-high to a grasshopper. Mildred, would you come here and see how this boy has grown.”

We'd covered less than ten homes in twenty minutes, when Peanut ripped off my mask and threw it in the bushes. Within fifty houses we were back on track and finished the first night at the strike of nine.

Shortly before six the next evening, Peanut appeared at our doorstep, his map of Danville in hand. "We hit the west side of town tonight. Fewer houses, the lots are farther apart. We'll have to hurry."

The west end of town was where the hoodlums lived. After three hours Peanut and I had each amassed a bagful of candy, but were mugged in an alleyway by Danny Millardo and his band of thugs. Long before Osama bin Laden ever thought of terrorizing anyone, Danny Millardo and his minions were seasoned hands. They bent our bicycle rims, then dumped our candy on the ground, pawing through it looking for Clark bars—Danny's favorite—stomping on the candy, then on us.

"This is my part of town," Danny said, twisting our ears. "Stay out of it."

We staggered home, our ears throbbing, our bicycles striking off in one direction then another.

"I forgot all about Danny Millardo," Peanut said after a few blocks. "This has thrown off our whole plan."

Ever since then, I have calculated the odds of tyranny into my plans.

"What happened to you?" my father asked when I walked through the door.

"Danny Millardo beat me up and stole my candy," I said.

"You should have popped him in the chops," my father said.

My father was forever advising me to pop someone in the chops, never considering the possibility I might be popped back. Then he launched into a story about when he was a kid and a bully had hit him. "I popped him right in the chops and that took care of it," he said, finishing his story with a flourish. Dad had a repository of childhood stories upon which he could draw at a moment's notice to fit any occasion, most of them ending with his popping someone in the chops.

The next day was Halloween, and the trick-or-treaters were out in full force, slowing us down. Peanut and I covered the north side of town, moving from one house to another, workmanlike, but fell short of our goal. We caught a brief glimpse of Danny Millardo, operating outside his turf, shaking down a group of ghosts, but we hurried past and escaped his notice. That night I ate several pounds of chocolate and woke up the next morning with severe diarrhea, my colon ratcheted into overdrive by all the caffeine I'd consumed. I stayed home from school, which knocked me out of the Halloween marathon.

The fifth night was a bust, candywise. By then the good candy had been dispensed and people were reduced to giving us the dregs from their pantries, mostly fruit and candy corn, both of which I despised. I especially hated candy corn and would have happily spit on the grave of George Renninger, the man who'd invented it in the 1880s.

Nevertheless, candy corn was wildly popular in my youth. It was cheap, selling in fifty-five-gallon drums at the Danner's Five and Dime or could be delivered directly to your home, dumped down the coal chute and into your cellar. It had a shelf life of decades and was routinely held over from one Halloween to the next. Peanut loved candy corn and persuaded his aunt to use it as the key ingredient in a variety of dishes and desserts—candy corn pie, candy corn cake, candy corn cookies, and candy corn pizza. In the months following Halloween, he happily subsisted on a steady diet of it, his skin turning a waxy orangey-yellow. After a few years, he began to resemble candy corn, wide on the bottom tapering to a point at his peanuty head.

Within a month most of my candy had gone stale. I was left with a heap of root beer barrels gone sticky. The next year I confined my trick-or-treating to two days and, preferring quality over quantity, concentrated my attentions on the north side of town where the rich people lived, far from the likes of Danny Millardo—who, true to his thuggish character, grew up and moved to Wall Street.

Chapter 12

Old Men

Nearly thirty years have passed since my growing-up years, and my fondest recollections are of things that should have killed me, chief among them swimming in the toxic pools of White Lick Creek. The creek had its origins nine miles north of town in the drain tiles of Indiana farmland, where two anonymous ditches joined at Harry Helbig's farm to form the White Lick Creek, which wound through the town park, under Highway 36, past the Texaco, skirting the field behind our home. By the time it reached town, it was a full-fledged creek, wide and swift-running in early spring, collecting in stagnant pools in August, waterbugs juking across its surface.

The creek was the only geographical feature of note in Danville, and we kids flocked to it the way other kids with more interesting terrain gathered at their wonders. It was our mountain and beach rolled into one, the topic of conversation during the rainy spells, townspeople speculating how high it might go, recalling past floods with a nostalgic yearning, the stories and hazards expanding with the years.

Harve Ellis, the park superintendent, was the official creek historian, the man people turned to when a flood argument needed settling. A walking repository of water lore, he tracked the creek's rise and fall the way investors studied the Dow Jones. He'd installed a white post behind the maintenance shed, at the edge of the creek. At the flood's peak, he would sail forth in a rowboat, paintbrush in hand, navigating the boat alongside the post, dabbing paint at the high-water mark, penciling in the date above the smear of paint. The current would invariably sweep him away and he would start over, landing the boat, then dragging it upstream and launching into the current, sometimes three or four times, such was his determination to document the event.

Peanut and I would watch him from the bridge, Peanut yelling advice, all of it singularly unhelpful, me imploring the Lord Jesus to spare Harve's life.* Stories circulated around town of children and old people being swept away by

* I had a vested interest in Harve's survival. In addition to working in the park, he was our town's wart man. Growing up, I'd been plagued with warts, growing in thick profusion on my hands. I'd been to a doctor and had them burnt off, which only caused them to grow back thicker, like prairie grass after a fire. When I was fourteen, Harve bought my warts, giving me fifty cents for the whole lot of them. Within two weeks they were gone, and I've been wart-free ever since.

the White Lick, their bloated bodies found days later downstream. This only increased our fascination with the creek, and we spent much of our young lives in it or on it.

On hot summer days late in the month, when money was scarce and the cost of swimming in the town pool prohibitive, Suds, Peanut, my brothers, and I would hike to the swimming hole just above the wastewater treatment plant. I shudder now to think of the lethal stew of chemicals present in the White Lick when we played there. As I write this, these many years later, I suspect a variety of malignant tumors are forming in my body, in the innermost reaches of my organs, and that I will end my life in wretched misery.

We spent countless afternoons at the creek, stripping down to our skivvies, swimming, then lying in the grass to dry off while Suds fantasized about various scenarios.

"What would you do if Denise Turner showed up here one day and took off her clothes right in front of us?" he would ask.

I know what I would have done—I would have wet my pants and run for home, but I didn't dare say so. Like most boys, I was terrified of girls, understood nothing about them, and avoided them whenever possible. Never in the memory of anyone I knew had a girl ever taken off her clothes in front of anyone, but that didn't stop Suds's creekside speculations.

We would discuss the many options available to us in the event Denise Turner were to disrobe in our presence, then we would return home, eat lunch, and go to Logan's Mobil to rummage around in the junk heap behind the gas station. We'd look for inner tubes we could salvage and turn into rafts, tubes with slow leaks that would get us a mile or two downstream before sinking. We would pump the inner tubes full of air, then run to the creek before they went flat, floating past the wastewater treatment plant and under the haunted bridge, past Johnson's farm, before washing up two miles south of town and walking home on Cartersburg Road.

Halfway to town, at the bottom of the Cartersburg Road hill, lived a man named Cowboy Landon in circumstances we boys considered ideal—a lean-to with no electricity or running water. He and his wife had squatted there for years, their shack crowded against the road, a pipe emerging from the hillside to supply them with water. Cowboy Landon was a nice guy, but rather unconventional, and worked odd jobs around town.

Cowboy's wife wore a wedding ring with a fake diamond, which she told us was real and worth millions, so we thought they were rich.

"What we ought to do," Suds said one day after we'd visited Cowboy and his wife, "is knock her on the head and steal her ring. I bet we could get five hundred dollars for it."

Five hundred dollars was the most money Suds could imagine. He would often come up with some scheme to make us rich, all of them netting exactly five hundred dollars.

"You moron," Peanut told Suds. "If they had a ring worth five hundred dollars, you think they'd be living in that dump? Don't be stupid."

"Maybe they live like that so people won't know they're rich and rob them," Suds said.

I sided with Suds, suspecting they were crazy rich, that their shack sat on top of a vault full of money.

If they had wealth, they were masterful at hiding it. They didn't own a car. Cowboy rode a red bicycle into town to the store, his groceries in a set of baskets that straddled his rear tire, raccoon tails dangling from his handlebars.

He and his wife apparently ate a lot of raccoon, and one fall day, when we'd stopped to visit, they invited us to join them for a raccoon dinner. "It tastes like chicken," she told us, spearing a chunk of gray-brown meat and presenting it to us. We declined her offer, but she was insistent. "You can eat it with just about anything," she said. "We like it in a stew, but you can have it with dumplings too. Squirrels taste good that way too. Cowboy, he can eat four or five squirrels at a time." She looked at Cowboy and beamed. He smiled modestly.

"Would they be eating squirrels and raccoons if they were rich?" Peanut asked Suds on the way home. "Don't be an idiot."

Across the road and up the hill from Cowboy lived Ralph Huber. Ralph was crazier than a bedbug, one of these guys you see on the news who shows up at work and shoots twelve people. Ralph's weapon of choice was lawn mower blades. He had a volatile temper, which caused children to taunt him for entertainment. Ralph would pull a lawn mower blade from the trunk of his car and chase after the children, hurling the blade at them.

Ralph had an inexhaustible supply of lawn mower blades. Every spring, our old blade being dented and dulled, I would provoke Ralph until he threw a blade at me that fit our mower. Even now, I recall the blade's boomerang flight, turning end over end, the faint whoosh as it sailed past my ear, nicking the lobe.

In all the years Ralph and I battled, he never caught me. I now believe that is the way he preferred it, that it was the chase he savored, not the capture, so he held back. To catch me would have altered the game, would have deviated from the script. Like the dog that finally catches a car, Ralph wouldn't have known what to do with me.

Ralph knew the mind of adolescent boys well and kept girlie magazines on the dashboard of his car, his way of baiting the trap. Teenage boys would reach in and snatch them from the car, and Ralph would leap out from behind a bush, swinging a lawn mower blade in wide arcs. It wasn't unusual to see a boy running through town carrying a *Playboy*, with Ralph on his heels slashing away. It had an unsettling effect on me. In my formative years, I associated nudity with mutilation and wore underwear even when I showered.

Parents liked Ralph, since he served as an example of what we might become if we didn't do our homework. "You want to be like Ralph Huber?" my mother would ask. "You keep ignoring your schoolwork and you'll be just like him." My mother lacked even the slightest insight into the psyche of a typical teenage boy. We considered Ralph's life idyllic. He lived in a shack in the woods, had a carload of girlie magazines, and wasn't weighed down by regular employment. At Career Day in high school, the girls wanted to be nurses or teachers or some other useful vocation. Mr. O'Brien, our guidance counselor, would smile and commend the girls for their earnestness.

"What do you want to be?" he asked Suds.

"I haven't decided," he said. "I either want to be like Ralph Huber or be a photographer for *Playboy*." Every boy in the room laughed until snot blew out our noses. Suds was a hoot.

Ralph had a brother named Lenny who lived in the Hotel Jones above Meazel Jewelry. Lenny did odd jobs around town, mostly tending yards. In the winter, Ralph moved into town to live with Lenny. By spring, they had tired of one another and would bicker, two old bachelors with loose dentures yelling incoherently, the sound of clacking teeth settling over the town square, the sign that winter was over. Ralph would migrate back to his shack on Cartersburg Road, cool down over the summer, and move back into town the next fall, taking his meals at the Coffee Cup Restaurant, clearing out the place whenever he entered, so foul was his odor. A zone opened around him wherever he went, people suddenly finding a reason to depart, remembering an important task back home that required their immediate attention.

When the Hotel Jones closed, Lenny went to live in the county home, up the hill and across Main Street from White Lick Creek. Sometime in the early '80s, he went weak in the head. It took awhile for people to notice, Lenny being a bit eccentric to begin with. He would escape from the county home and wander about town, visiting the people whose lawns he'd tended, stopping now and then to weed a flowerbed. On a winter day, he stumbled into the White Lick Creek, downstream from Harve Ellis's measuring post, and drowned. The police found his body the next day, resting up against a log, frozen, another story to add to the already considerable body of creek lore.

Chapter 13

My Many Shames

In 1878 our town appropriated the Central Normal College from Ladoga, Indiana. Its president, a Mr. William French Harper, was twenty-three years old, brilliant, but impulsive. He moved the college to Danville in the middle of a spring night. The following November he disappeared. When he returned home a year later, he claimed to have been abducted by Indians and held hostage in Wyoming before stealing a pony and escaping. His explanation was greeted with skepticism. It was the consensus of the townspeople that a woman was involved. The next year Harper moved to Los Angeles, became a Baptist minister, and wooed hundreds of women to the Lord.

The college died in 1952, but not before graduating sixty thousand teachers, some of whom tried to teach me. Our town inherited the campus and used it for a high school until 1973, when it became our junior high. The school was four blocks from our home, up Broadway to Wayne Street, across Main, past the Victory Bell to the school.* I would detour two blocks to Logan's Mobil each morning to buy ten pieces of Bazooka bubble gum. When I got to school I discreetly chewed them, then stuck the wad beneath my desk, adding to the mass of calcified gum clinging to its underside like barnacles to a boat.

Junior high school was a study in humiliation. Each day presented fresh opportunities for embarrassment and degradation. The tender oversight of elementary school was dispensed with, the brutality of life squarely faced. This was especially apparent in Mr. Johnson's eighth grade P.E. class, where we had to do the two things designed to strike fear into the heart of any adolescent boy—shower nude in front of others, and learn to dance.

Of the two, the showers were worse—standing naked among your peers while the football players snapped you with a towel and laughed at your winkie. Dancing ran a close second. In anticipation of the junior high dance, Mrs. Dollens, the girls' P.E. teacher, borrowed a phonograph from Mrs. McNeff in the library, trooped the girls down to the gymnasium, and seated them on the bleachers. The boys milled

* The Victory Bell was donated by the Scientific Club, Class of 1910, to be rung after sporting victories. It was seldom heard.

around, studying the girls like farmers inspecting horses, looking over their teeth, scrutinizing their hocks for slewfoot.

The protocol, I soon grasped, was to select from among the trove of beauties the one perfect specimen with whom to dance. Then, in order to avoid first-hand rejection, have your best friend ask for the pleasure of her company on your behalf.

"Who do you want to dance with?" Tim Hadley asked me.

"Jane Martin," I said, taking care not to select a girl so stratospherically popular I would face rejection, but not so homely I would be embarrassed. It was a fine line to tread. Tim petitioned Jane on my behalf. She eyed me warily, then nodded her head in agreement, though with little enthusiasm. Since my overtures to girls had customarily been met with scorn, her indifference was a welcome improvement.

The rest of the class paired off. There were more boys than girls, so Roger Varble and Billy Gibbs were forced to dance with one another, a humiliation from which they never recovered.

The only dance I knew was the waltz, from watching old movies with my dad. Apparently, Jane Martin hadn't watched the same movies. I put my right arm on the small of her back and inadvertently touched the clasp of her bra.

"What are you doing?" she asked, shrinking back, her voice cold.

"Dancing," I said, helpfully.

"You pervert!" Jerry Sipes said, punching me in the arm. "You're not supposed to touch 'em."

Jane told Mrs. Dollens she was sick, spent the rest of the hour in the bathroom, and didn't speak to me again until our twenty-year high school reunion. I had a way of driving girls to the restroom. Jane's reaction was consistent with all the girls I knew, each of whom had informed me they were perfectly content without me in their lives.

Junior high was miserable in other ways. Mrs. Disney had been the school cook for years, employing local farmwives to prepare a veritable feast each day for our pleasant ingestion. But she retired and the school switched to government food left over from World War II. It had sat for years in a government warehouse in New Jersey before being delivered to our school in a semi, the diesel fumes mingling with the food, forming a malignant stew. I've watched lunch scenes in old jailhouse movies that were eerily reminiscent of junior high school—beaten-down people standing in a sullen line while hard-bitten lifers slung great blobs of fly-specked gruel onto our plates.

After lunch, we were permitted outside to stroll in the cemetery next to the school, where the town's founders were buried. Suds Norton and I would walk up and down the quiet rows, reading the names, imagining those brave pioneers six feet beneath us, the men in their coonskin caps, the women in their bonnets and petticoats.

Suds would speculate out loud about what the women had looked like in their petticoats. That would occupy our minds until the bell rang and it was time for science with Mr. McClelland, who was to education what Genghis Khan was to gracious living. He made no secret about his motivation for teaching—summers off. His ignorance was so vast as to be breathtaking. Even now, thirty-five years down the road, errors he planted long ago surface, like a bullet lodged in a soldier's head sneezed out years later. For decades I labored under the notion that an electron was a vacuum cleaner brand, that protons were essential to a healthy diet, and neutrons replaced old trons.

My venture into science was redeemed every Friday when Mr. McClelland sent Tim Hadley and me to the janitor's room in the basement to siphon distilled water from a fifty-five gallon drum into four large pickle jars. For reasons unknown, he settled on Tim and me early on, never extending that privilege to anyone else. The teachers' Coke machine sat just inside the janitor's room. We would deposit a quarter, open the slender door, survey the selection, then pull a bottle of pop from the cold innards of the machine, nursing it down while the distilled water tinkled from the drum into the pickle jars. It felt deliciously sinful to be drinking a soda while our peers labored under the burden of Mr. McClelland's sorry tutelage.

Tim's father, Ralph, was the school janitor. He holed up in his basement room, his feet propped on the pail of sawdust he kept handy in the event of an outbreak of vomiting. A squat, bowlegged man, Ralph Hadley attended the Quaker meeting every Sunday. His wife played the piano and he led singing in a high, reedy voice underneath the picture of George Fox, the founder of Quakerism. George Fox was grimacing, as if the congregation had hit a clinker.

By then, I had grown weary of Catholicism and was eyeing the Quakers, attending every now and then with Tim. The Quakers wore their religion lightly and were especially kind to junior high children, who they sensed were troubled enough as it was, so didn't add to their already considerable burdens. If they thought I was headed to hell, they never said so, while the Baptists were prone to elaborate. The Baptist children would read their Bibles during study hall, poring through the book of Leviticus, then glancing my direction and frowning. It was clear where I stood with them, especially after word got out that I had touched Jane Martin's bra.

One of the Baptists, an earnest boy named Daryl, showed me passages in the Bible about the Christians rising from their graves on Judgment Day, which he knew for a fact was just around the corner. I certainly didn't want to miss that and made sure my desk in math class overlooked the cemetery so I could see their resurrection firsthand. I imagined the earth buckling, the gravestones toppling over, the wooden coffins pushing up through the soil and opening, the pioneers stepping out of their caskets, shaking the dust from their garments, and ascending to heaven.

"But not all of them," Daryl said, "just the Baptists."

We had story problems in Mrs. Cole's math class, all of them involving trains, which no one rode anymore. I wondered why there weren't any story problems about Judgment Day. "If 3,254 Catholics and Baptists are buried in a cemetery, and 38 percent go to heaven on Judgment Day, how many Baptists were in the cemetery?" It would have been a trick question, since Catholics and Baptists weren't buried in the same cemetery, lest God get confused on the Day of Reckoning and accidentally resurrect an unworthy soul.

Of course, I knew from science class that bodies couldn't rise in the air without adequate thrust. The Bible was silent on the subject of propulsion, which I pointed out to Daryl, but his mind was made up on the matter and he wouldn't budge.

"With God all things are possible," he said. And that was that.

I wanted to believe all things were possible with God, but God wasn't knocking himself out proving it to me. My prayers for divine intervention went consistently unanswered. I'd started small, so as not to tax the Lord, asking for a date with Denise Turner. But she never agreed, in spite of my fervent supplications. I asked Daryl his thoughts on the matter. It was his opinion that God had turned off the spigot of blessings because we'd been dancing in P.E. According to Daryl, God was death on dancing.

While God and I saw eye-to-eye on the dancing question, we agreed on little beyond that. We'd gotten off to a poor start at St. Mary's Catholic Church when it turned out everything I enjoyed was a sin—daydreaming about Denise Turner, contemplating marriage to Denise Turner, getting Denise Turner in a family way. Yahweh, I knew, was death on such matters. In junior high, I began to seek out a kinder, gentler deity, preferably in a church with pretty girls, which is how I ended up among the Quakers. (I'll tell you more about this later.) It is somewhat disconcerting, thirty-five years later, to realize my career as a pastor was launched by hormones, but the ways of the Lord are mysterious and not for mortals to understand. That is precisely what William French Harper said when he'd returned home after being kidnapped by the Indians. But everyone saw right through him, as they saw through me, we minister-types being too transparent for our own good.

•

Chapter 14

My Sporadic Uprisings

When I was growing up, a boy could wreak havoc without his parents hauling him to a doctor to be drugged. Indeed, youthful rebellion was expected and if sporadic uprisings didn't occur, parents assumed the worst—their boy lacked the vital spark and his days were numbered. My brothers and I took full advantage of this relaxed oversight and waged campaigns of terror that left our town's citizenry deeply traumatized, if not permanently scarred.

My father was an unwitting accomplice in most of our misdeeds, providing the means, inspiration, or both. Though his vocation was selling bug spray, his passion was bartering. He returned home each evening bearing various treasures he'd gotten in exchange for bug poison. His finest acquisition, the one that shines brightest in my memory, was a female mannequin.

Aside from her wooden personality, she was perfect in every way—agreeable, shapely, always ready for a good time, and even-tempered.

Doug was unusually modest for a teenager and suggested we clothe her. Our sister was away at college, so we raided her closet for clothing, dressing her in clothes she was no longer able to wear since becoming a Baptist—a miniskirt, halter top, and socks with individual toes in them that dangled empty, the mannequin lacking digits. David scrounged up a woman's red wig from Suds Norton, who seemed curiously reluctant to part with it.

"What should we name her?" Glenn asked.

We batted names back and forth before settling on Ginger, of *Gilligan's Island* fame.

The first few days we did the usual things one does with a mannequin—dangled her legs out the car trunk, used her to moon passersby, arranged her in provocative poses under the streetlight in front of our house. But on a hot summer evening, in our second week with her, our association would reach a pinnacle in an event still talked about in our town.

A quarter mile south of our home, on the road out of town, was a railroad bridge whose arches rose high above the road. Like most old bridges, rumors swirled around it, chiefly that it was haunted, that during its construction in the early 1900s a worker had plunged to his death and could be heard screaming each night.

My cousin Matt had come for his annual visit from southern Indiana. We'd soon exhausted all avenues of entertainment and were seated on the front porch early one evening, mulling over possible leisure activities.

"What we ought to do," Matt said, "is throw her off the bridge in front of a car."

This seemed to the rest of us an exceptional idea, a fitting end to the day. We lashed her to the back of Doug's Sting Ray and pedaled the quarter mile to the bridge, hiding our bicycles in the rushes along the creek bank, and hauling her to the top. Matt carried her over his shoulder, her limbs sticking out at hard right angles, as if she were stiff with rigor mortis.

"The first thing we do is tie a rope around her," Matt said, fashioning a noose around her slender neck, his hand grazing her wooden breast.

"Knock it off, you pervert," Glenn said, slapping Matt's hand away.

We sat with Ginger in the dark, watching toward town for the stab of headlights.

"Here we go," Doug said, the whine of an engine audible in the distance.

The car approached the bridge, Matt cinched the noose tight around Ginger's neck, and pushed her off into the black night. She came to a snapping halt at windshield level, swinging back and forth in front of the headlights, her wig a blood-red smear, her eyes wide and vacant, staring at the driver.

"Crap," Matt said. "It's a cop." He hauled Ginger up, hand over hand, her miniskirt bunched at her feet, her halter top down around her waist.

It was not just any cop. It was Charley Williams, the chief of police, on his evening rounds.

Chief Williams peered upward into the bowels of the bridge. He was well past sixty-five and not inclined to climb up after us. He retrieved the megaphone from the trunk of his car, aimed it toward the bridge, and yelled, "You come down from there or I'll send the dog up."

We began to convulse with silent laughter. Danville's police dog was an arthritic German Shepherd that had to be lifted out of Charley's car. It also had a sinus condition and couldn't smell a rose an inch from its nose. It had been trained in Germany, didn't know a word of English, which didn't matter since it was also deaf. The town had purchased the dog years before for two hundred dollars. We'd had a fundraiser at the school to buy him. Every child brought in a quarter, except for Bobby Darnell, whose family lived over the hardware store and was poor. He dropped in a washer.

Charley Williams was an inveterate whistler, constantly at it, the only man I ever knew who could whistle and talk at the same time. He poked around the bushes—whistling, whistling, whistling—then shined his flashlight into the rushes along the creek. We lay in the arches of the bridge, death-still. My father was president of the town board and technically Charley Williams's boss, but we took no comfort in that. My father had told us countless times that if our activities ever drew the attention of the police, we would spend the rest of our lives in jail before he bailed us out. Eventually, Charley grew tired and left. We loaded Ginger back onto Doug's bicycle and rode home, inordinately pleased with ourselves for escaping detection.

Over the course of that summer we had much wholesome fun with Ginger, until an accident with a truck resulted in the loss of her legs. We carried her to the end of the driveway on trash day, where she was loaded onto Doc Foster's pickup truck and hauled to the dump. It was an ignoble end for someone who had brought us such pleasure, and all these years later I still feel guilty we hadn't given Ginger the Christian burial she'd deserved.

That same summer my father had gotten it into his head that we had too much time on our hands and were at risk for juvenile delinquency. So he traded several cases of bug spray for a hundred tomato plants and had my brothers and me plant them in the garden behind our barn. No calculator exists that can accurately extrapolate the tons of tomatoes generated by a hundred plants. By July, we had wheelbarrow loads of tomatoes each day and were eating them at every meal, in combinations limited only by my mother's imagination—tomato soup, tomato salad, tomato pie, tomato juice, tomato stew, tomato loaf, tomato hotdish, tomato casserole, tomato goulash, and Great God Almighty, on a hot Sunday afternoon, homemade tomato ice cream.

My father was delighted. "The land is feeding us," he marveled one evening over a slice of warm tomato cake.

"Next year I'll see if I can't trade for some zucchini seeds."

We ate so many tomatoes our fingernails turned red.

"If I have to eat another tomato, I think I'll puke," I said to Peanut one summer afternoon. I'd had a tomato and jelly sandwich for lunch that day and it was threatening to surface.

Peanut sat quietly, pondering my dilemma.

"What we have to do," he said finally, "is get rid of the tomatoes quicker than your mother can cook them." Then, in a conspiratorial whisper, he told me his plan.

We met at the tomato patch that night after dark. Peanut, Suds Norton, and I. Peanut was carrying several large buckets, which we filled in no time.

"Follow me," he said, seizing hold of a bucket.

Peanut struck off through the night, up the street, avoiding the streetlights, making his way through the Martins' yard and down their back hill to the Laundromat. The Laundromat sat on U.S. 36, our town's Main Street. Built into a hill, the rear roof of the Laundromat sat a scant four feet off the ground. Peanut scrambled onto the roof.

"Hand me the tomatoes," he said. Suds and I lifted the buckets onto the roof, then climbed up ourselves.

"What we have to do," Peanut said, "is hide behind the sign and throw the tomatoes out onto Main Street. Aim for the cars. When the tomatoes hit their windshields, they'll think they ran over somebody."

For reasons I still can't fathom, this struck me as a perfectly laudable idea, and we began launching tomatoes from the Laundromat roof.

"Throw 'em like grenades. Like they do in the movies," Peanut said, lobbing a tomato high over the sign. It arced above the parking lot, narrowly missing a Chevrolet before splatting in the middle of Main Street. We dialed in the sights, and our accuracy improved. Tomatoes glazed across windshields, leaving a meaty, seedy smear.

Traffic snarled to a halt. Charley Williams arrived in his patrol car. He lifted the police dog out of the back seat, then studied the red gore on the road, trying to determine whether it was flora or fauna. The dog lapped up the tomatoes, indifferent to the vegetable carnage that had been visited upon the civilian population.

Charley walked around the building, whistling, and said, "Come on out, boys. I know you're somewhere around here."

We lay on the roof behind the *One Hour Martinizing* sign, not budging, knowing capture would mean our demise. This time we'd gone too far. It had been one thing to toss a mannequin off a bridge, which, though distressing to passersby, was technically not illegal. But throwing a tomato at a car was a crime, perhaps even a felony, which could result in our being sent to the Indiana Boys School, where the highlight of our week would be playing checkers with the old men from the Quaker church who visited on Thursday evenings.*

* Quaker men, I would later learn after becoming one, are big believers in the redemptive powers of checkers. Our response to youthful transgression is invariably the same—"Hey, you young whippersnapper, bet you can't beat me in a game of checkers." Then, while seated across from the offender, we'll inundate the delinquent with cracker-barrel moralisms until, bored out of his skull and ready to slash his wrists, he promises to walk the straight and narrow. It generally takes about ten minutes.

Charley Williams walked up to the Laundromat, the police dog limping along beside him. He rattled the door, checking the lock. "Think anyone's in there?" he asked the dog. We stopped breathing and listened closely, hoping the dog would say, "Looks empty to me. Let's go home." Instead, Charley circled the building, shining his flashlight, whistling, whistling, whistling. The dog went back to eating the tomatoes, looking up occasionally and licking his chops, which glistened tomato-red in the streetlight, like Cujo in the Stephen King book.

After a while, Charley hefted his dog back into the cruiser and drove off. We stayed on the roof, lying on our backs, looking up at the stars and contemplating our sins.

"That was the most fun I've had since Denise Turner's bikini top fell off at the pool last week," Suds Norton said.

"Wow!" Peanut said. "Did you see her boobies?"

"Yep."

"What did they look like?" Peanut asked.

Suds thought for a moment, smiling fondly at the memory. "Tomatoes," he said. "Nice, ripe tomatoes."

I knew exactly what he meant. Everything I saw that summer reminded me of tomatoes.

At the height of the tomato harvest, my father traded bug spray for six dozen Ball canning jars. "Now we can have tomatoes year-round," he said, positively giddy with joy. The next morning, after he'd left for work, my mother and I hid the jars in the coal bins behind the furnace. For the next several days, Dad wandered around the house, peering into closets and scratching his head. "Now where did I put those jars? Has anyone seen the jars?" Fortunately, my father was easily distracted. After a while something else would catch his interest and he'd forget about the canning jars.

The next week all the tomato plants were ripped from the ground, thrown into a pile, doused with fuel, and set on fire. We never found out who did it, though Glenn seemed inordinately pleased by their destruction and smelled suspiciously of kerosene.

With the tomato curse now lifted, my brothers and I turned our attention toward more noble pursuits. As is often the case, the next grand adventure fell into our laps when we weren't even looking for it. It was a rainy summer day. We'd gotten on my mother's nerves, and she'd banished us from the house. Exiled, we took up refuge with Suds and Peanut in the loft of the barn where our father stored his cases of bug spray.

We were draped across the boxes, discussing Denise Turner's many qualities, when Doug began reading the label on a can of bug spray. "Listen to this," he said. "Contents under pressure. Do not puncture or incinerate."

"What's *incinerate* mean?" Suds asked.

"It means it can't be used in a prison," I said.

"I had an uncle in prison," Suds said. "He never said anything about bug spray not being allowed."

"Maybe it's a new rule," I said.

This led to a lengthy discussion about prison and who among our acquaintances seemed destined to land there. "Probably Danny Millardo," Suds said.

"I wonder what happens when you puncture a can of bug spray," Suds asked, returning to the subject at hand.

"It probably explodes," I said.

"So it's like a bomb," Doug said, and with that insight, our day was transformed.

"Set it on the floor and I'll shoot it with my slingshot," Suds said.

"Are you crazy?" Peanuts said, ever ready with a historical tidbit. "The shrapnel will kill us. Do you know how many people died from shrapnel in World War II? Over a hundred million, then they stopped counting. Set the can on the ground and we'll drop a rock on it from the window."

We went in search of a rock of sufficient size to split open a can of bug spray, then laid the can on its side underneath the barn's second-story window. Since it had been mostly Doug's idea, we let him have the first turn. We crowded around the window while Doug sighted down the rock, like a WWII bombardier zeroing in on a Nazi gun factory. "Bomb's away," he said, dropping the stone.

It struck the canister dead center. The can exploded, lifting high into the air and whirling about, spewing bug spray in a wide, poisonous arc. We stood at the window, dumbstruck, then turned to gaze at the cases of bug spray filling the hayloft, the realization of our newfound power slowly dawning.

"Our very own bombs," Suds said, his voice trembly with awe. "Just think what we can do."

Over the next several days, a barrage of bug bombs were detonated behind our barn. Cans were shot at, impaled, imploded, and exploded, releasing such vast quantities of toxins that every bug within a mile was gassed, the topsoil contaminated, and the humans struck with an asthmatic hack. There was, and remains to this day, a white, cracked-earth dead zone thirty feet out from the barn in all directions.

The following Saturday my father wandered around the barn, peering into the stalls and hayloft, and scratching his head. "I seem to be out of bug spray," he said. "Have you seen any?"

"Last time I saw the bug spray, it was next to the canning jars," I said.

"Aha!" he said. "I'll check the attic."

Within a few minutes, he'd found his old army uniform and was reminiscing about his days at Fort Knox, Kentucky.

My brothers and I shared many exciting summers, but our season with Ginger the mannequin surpassed them all. My cousin Matt continued to visit us for a week each July, but never topped his creativity with Ginger at the bridge. That evening still shines in the Polaroid hues of memory. As for Peanut and Suds, we would share other vegetable holocausts over the years, but our tomato summer remained the crowning glory of our felonious youth.

Chapter 15

Bicycle Glories

The Schwinn Varsity ten-speed bicycle was invented in 1960, but I didn't get mine until June 16, 1975, when my mother drove me to A-1 Cyclery in Indianapolis and I plunked down $138.78 for a green Schwinn Varsity (Model #124, Serial # DL545900). I had been promised a bicycle in lieu of a school trip to Washington, D.C., but my parents never paid me back. I still have the receipt and bill them monthly, but it appears they've stiffed me, a sordid little detail I intend to mention when I deliver their eulogies.

Floyd Jennings owned the Schwinn bicycle shop in our town, in the basement of the Abstract and Title Building next to Vern Hedge's barbershop. Floyd was prickly tempered, prone to outbursts, and my mother refused to do business with him. "I will not give that man my hard-earned money," she said. Mom was dogmatic about few things, but Floyd Jennings was one of them. I was not that particular. I would have bought my Schwinn Varsity from Adolf Hitler if he had been in the bike business.

So on a Monday morning in 1975, thumbing our noses at convention, we drove the Plymouth Valiant to the city to buy my Varsity. The bike didn't fit in the trunk, so I rode it home, my mother following behind me, flashing her hazard lights. We were on Highway 40, which crossed the nation from Atlantic City to San Francisco. I imagined I was traversing the country on my bike, raising money for legless orphans. When I reached San Francisco, I would appear together on *The Phil Donahue Show*, where I would smile modestly and say it was nothing, a walk in the park, an unfortunate turn of phrase when discussing amputees, but the audience would clap anyway and Phil Donahue would weep. A billionaire would be watching that day and, inspired by my altruism, send me a million dollars.

I'd had my green Varsity several months when Tim Trapp and Frank Freeman, whose wretched lives had also been transformed by the purchase of Schwinn Varsitys, suggested we bicycle the fifty miles to Turkey Run State Park and camp overnight. Though we were only fourteen, our parents allowed it. Indeed, they seemed pleased at the prospect of being shed of us for a weekend.

We left on a cold, rainy autumn morning. We had packed brownies, a radio, a book of crossword puzzles, harmonicas, pocket knives, and a BB pistol, but no rain gear. Within two miles we were soaked to the bone and shivering uncontrollably, on the verge of hypothermia. We rode single file, with Tim taking up the rear, calling out advice like a coxswain in a racing shell—"Downshift!" "Pothole!" "Turn right!" "Dead raccoon!"

Tim was well-versed on every hazard and prior to our departure had delivered a lecture on the hidden dangers of wet railroad tracks. "Perpendicular," he warned us. "You must cross railroad tracks perpendicularly."

Frank and I looked at one another, confused.

"What's *perpendicular*?" I asked Frank when Tim had walked away.

"Beats me."

We'd ridden twenty miles when we approached our first set of railroad tracks at the base of a long hill. We streaked down the incline toward the tracks, which angled across the road.

"Perpendicular!" yelled Tim, far behind us, "Cross the tracks perpendicularly!"

I recall Frank's crash in the grayed tones of memory, like a World War II newsreel. His front tire hitting the first railroad track, slick with rain, the bike sliding sideways, Frank sailing through the air and landing on his knees, in the convenient posture of prayer, then toppling over in a heap, his skin flayed by gravel.

Tim and I stood over him. "Don't move him," I said. "He could have a broken neck. If we move him, he'll die."

"How do you know that?"

"I saw it on TV, on *Emergency*," I said. "This guy wrecked and they moved him and his neck snapped, just like that. His head was flopping to one side. It killed him. They might as well have shot him."

I had been an ardent fan of *Emergency*, viewing it faithfully every Saturday evening, and had amassed a tremendous store of medical trivia.

Tim nudged Frank with his foot. "I told him perpendicular."

"You certainly did," I agreed. "He should have known better."

"This rain is certainly a blessing," Tim said. "It appears to be washing away his blood."

Frank came to after a few minutes, and we resumed our trip. The rain continued the next thirty miles as the temperature fell. When we arrived at the state park, I remembered Tim phoning the night before, reminding me to bring the tent. Unfortunately, in my haste to leave that morning, I'd forgotten it. I wondered how to tell them, and decided the rugged he-man approach would work best.

"If we were real men, we'd build a shelter from pine boughs instead of using a tent," I said.

"You go right ahead," said Tim. "But I'm sleeping in a tent."

"I'm sure there's a cave around here we can sleep in," I persisted. "That's what Daniel Boone did on his bicycle trips."

"Daniel Boone didn't have a bicycle," Tim said.

"Yeah, well, I don't have a tent. I forgot and left it at home."

Frank was slumped against a tree, lying in the mud, his wounds oozing blood.

I suggested we rent a room in the park inn. Frank groaned. He hated spending money.

We sat down under the tree next to Frank, splats of rain dropping on us from the leaves.

I asked Tim what he'd brought for supper.

"Brownies," he said.

Frank was in no condition to eat, so Tim and I split the brownies.

We pooled our money and stayed in the inn that night. We had spent all our money on the room, the brownies were gone, and we were down to one box of CoCo Wheats, a chocolaty grits-like breakfast food invented for prisoners.

I had remembered to bring a cookstove, which we fired up the next morning to cook our CoCo Wheats. Unfortunately, we burnt them, triggering the room's smoke alarm. The manager was at our door within seconds. Frank and Tim hid the stove, while I dumped the CoCo Wheats in the toilet, just before the manager peered into the bathroom, looking for fire, but spying the CoCo Wheats. I was standing next to the toilet, appearing somewhat distressed. "He doesn't feel well," Tim told the manager. "Spastic colon."

We departed shortly thereafter, at the manager's request. It was still raining. Within a few miles, Frank hit a patch of gravel on a turn and crashed again, landing in a roadside ditch.* After that trip, it would be years before he rode again, so deep were his emotional scars. As for Tim and me, we

* Ironically, Frank would graduate high school, attend college where he would study engineering, then work for a company involved in transportation safety.

were pleased to note that the Schwinn Varsity was so ruggedly constructed it could sustain wreck after wreck with scarcely a scratch.

That was the first of many trips I made that summer, launching forth on my Varsity to see the world, my provisions strapped to the rack over the rear wheel, lashed to the handlebars, or crammed into my bug backpack. My dietary needs were simple. I carried a case of Dinty Moore beef stew and nothing else. Riding a bike was hard work and I was constantly famished, stopping every three hours to fire up my small camping stove and warm a can of stew. When I was halfway through the case, roughly eighty miles from home, I would turn back, stopping a few hours outside Danville to consume the last of the Dinty Moore, then coasting the last mile on fumes. To this day, whenever I eat a can of Dinty Moore beef stew, I hear the rubbery whine of tire against the road and the click of the sprocket, feel the burn in my thighs, and the wind in my face.*

There were days when I entertained the notion of riding my bicycle to the Hormel Food Corporation in Austin, Minnesota, where Dinty Moore beef stew was made, but it was 530 miles away and would have required nearly ninety cans of beef stew, which I couldn't carry. Appeals to my father to vacation in Austin fell on deaf ears, even when I pointed out we could stop at the Hormel Chili plant in Beloit, Wisconsin, and see the world's largest can of chili.

---

* Between the time I moved from home at the age of nineteen and when I married at the age of twenty-three, I ate Dinty Moore twice a day. High in beta-carotene, it gave me superb vision, moist mucus membranes, and orange palms.

While my parents let me ride my bicycle long distances on busy state highways, they forbade me from riding my bicycle down Main Street, fearing I would be killed. Roughly four cars each day passed through our town. Dogs slept in the road for hours at a time, unmolested. But my parents viewed Main Street as the Highway of Death and Carnage. Every night at supper, my mother peered at me from across the table. "That wasn't you I saw on Main Street today, was it? I've told you before I don't want you riding your bike on Main Street."

"Wasn't me," I lied.

"You heard your mother," Dad would say. "Stay off Main Street."

"I was thinking of riding my bicycle up to the city this weekend and looping I-465," I would say a few moments later.

My mother would smile from across the table. "Oh, that sounds fun. Why don't you take your little brother with you?"

Who could figure parents?

Living nineteen miles from the Indianapolis 500, the kids in my neighborhood were obsessed with racing, though none of us had actually attended the race. Years before, while selling bug spray, my father had met Tony Hulman, the owner of the track, and they'd hit it off. Every spring, tickets to the race appeared in our mailbox. My father gave them to my cousin Matt, of mannequin fame.

"You wouldn't catch me dead up there," Dad said. "All that traffic. No thanks. You can have that mess. I don't want anything to do with it."

Every Memorial Day weekend, my brothers and I and our friends would listen to the 500 on the radio, it being blacked out on local television. When it was over we would stage a bicycle race, stretching out in a line in front of Suds Norton's house, a dozen of us arranged from one sidewalk to the other, a row of Schwinns, Raleighs, Vistas, and Peanut on his Huffy. Peanut swore by Huffys and would walk before riding anything else.

Suds's mother was our official starter. She would stand on the sidewalk, cigarette dangling from her mouth, scowling, while Peanut pumped away madly, inflating his bicycle tires until they nearly burst from the rim. Peanut believed the firmer the tire, the less of it would touch the road, minimizing resistance and giving him an advantage. As theories go, Peanut was correct. In practice, his tires were time bombs. Within the first block, he would hit a patch or pothole, and the tires would explode, catapulting him over the handlebars and into a tree.

"What the hell you thinkin'?" Mrs. Norton would yell after a few minutes of watching Peanut pump his tires. "I don't got all day. Get your butt on that bike and let's get going!"

We would spin our cranks around, positioning the right pedal at twelve o'clock for maximum thrust. Mrs. Norton would count to three, pausing between each number to draw on her cigarette, then hit the word *Go*, and we would hurl ourselves forward like Mario Andretti at the Speedway.

Our block was a half-mile around, so ten laps gave us a five-mile race. Unlike the 500, we were not constrained by rules. Cheating was permitted and encouraged. Our favorite tactic was to jam sticks in the spokes of the other riders, causing their bikes to come to a dead stop, flinging our competitors onto the road, where they would be struck down by the other riders and squished into the tar.

Without fail, the winner would be disputed, and the race would end in a fistfight in Suds's front yard, while his mother looked on from their front porch yelling advice. "Hit him in the nose, that'll teach him." She would take a long drag from her cigarette. "Yep," she would say to no one in particular, "a good shot to the nose will shut up just about anybody."

After the fight, I would run home, get my first-aid kit and patch up the loser, just as I'd learned from watching *Emergency*.

Several years later, my brothers and I would get our driver's licenses and race the same way, except in cars. Miraculously, none of us died. Then God, in that ironic way of the Divine, gave us children to show us how worrisome it could be when boys were long on wheels and short on brains.

Chapter 16

Mildred

In my fourteenth year, I received a letter from Mildred Harvey summoning me to her home. Mrs. Harvey lived four doors west of us. Her husband was in the nursing home, leaving her to keep up their home place. She was well into her seventies, weary of the effort, and looking for help. "Philip Gulley," the note read in shaky, old-lady handwriting, "I would like to hire you as my yard boy. Please come see me. Mildred Harvey."

I'd met Mildred Harvey shortly after we'd moved to Broadway Street. The first time we met, I called her Mrs. Harvey, as I had been taught to address my elders.

"I am a Quaker," she said. "We don't use titles. You may call me Mildred."

"Yes, ma'am."

"We don't say 'sir' or 'ma'am' either."

"Yes, Mildred."

Quakers, I concluded, were peculiar people.

I walked down the sidewalk to Mildred's home the next Sunday. She was seated on her front porch, in a wicker rocking chair, fanning herself with the newspaper.

"Hello, Mildred Harvey," I said.

"Hello, Philip Gulley. Please have a seat," she said, gesturing to her porch swing.

I mentioned receiving her note.

"Let's not discuss business on the Sabbath," she said, fanning herself. "It will keep until tomorrow."

For as long as I knew Mildred, she had strong ideas about proper Sabbath activity—no doing work, no speaking of work, no thinking of work. Card playing, however, was permissible, and she passed long summer hours on her front porch playing Solitaire.

We visited awhile, then I went home and returned the next morning. Mildred Harvey was clipping the hedge that ran along her driveway. After I greeted her, taking care not to offend her Quaker sensibilities, she asked if I wanted to mow her yard. Her home sat on two acres, which her husband had cut with an old-fashioned reel mower. She never mentioned why her husband was in the nursing home, but I suspected that pushing the lawn mower around their yard had finally broken him.

"You can use my lawn mower," she offered. "It's nice and quiet and doesn't use gas."

Mildred Harvey was not a fan of the internal combustion engine and was forever preaching against its use, as if it were a moral failure to employ motorized assistance.

"If you don't mind, I would prefer to use a gas mower," I said.

Mildred Harvey frowned. She didn't say anything, but I could tell I had slipped a notch in her estimation.

The Harveys had moved into the house fifty years earlier and had been hard at it ever since, planting flowers, bushes, and other annoyances to mow around. She showed me around the yard, pointing out various plants, expressing the hope that I wouldn't annihilate them with my out-of-control gasoline mower. I suggested we might begin by clear-cutting her yard, but my suggestions fell on deaf ears.

Everything I said to Mildred Harvey fell on deaf ears. She was hard of hearing, which impeded our ability to converse. One of our more memorable conversations happened the winter after I'd begun mowing her lawn. I had stopped by her house the day after Christmas, and was sitting in her front parlor, recounting my family's holiday.

"My mom got up early Christmas morning and made us Eggs Benedict Florentine," I said.

Mildred frowned. "You were under quarantine? That's a terrible way to spend Christmas." She humped her chair a scootch farther away from me.

"No, she made eggs," I yelled.

"Yes," Mildred said, "it was in your legs. Are you better now?"

"Much," I said.

Despite these occasional detours into choppy waters, Mildred and I would go on to form a long partnership.

After the tour of her yard, we moved to the porch to negotiate a price. I was inexperienced in such matters and accepted the first offer she made—twenty dollars a mowing. This was huge money. Twice as much as I was making delivering newspapers. That afternoon, I gave my two-week notice at the newspaper office and became Mildred Harvey's official yard boy.

With that much money at stake, I entertained the notion of quitting school and mowing full time. There were three men in our town who did yard work for a living: the previously mentioned Ralph and Lenny Huber, and a Mr. Kruller, who lived in a small yellow house next to the cemetery and wore dresses in the evenings.

Mr. Kruller was a perfect size 10. Women would have killed for his hips, which curved nicely without being too fleshy. He attributed his figure to lawn mowing, pushing the mower back and forth, day after summer day, the muscles firming, the pounds melting away. He never married, despite several proposals, one from Lenny Huber.

Mildred Harvey didn't appear to be giving her figure a second thought. She was generously proportioned, in a matronly sort of way, like Aunt Bee of Mayberry. Stepping into her house was akin to visiting my grandmother. Heavy drapes, lace tabletops, dark Victorian furniture like those on *The Addams Family*. Dust motes floated through the air, ignited by the odd shaft of window light.

Landing Mildred Harvey as a client vaulted me into the stratosphere of the Quaker widows' circuit. Within a few weeks, I was swamped by Quaker women needing help. The benefits were excellent—homemade cookies out the wazoo and the inside track to their granddaughters—but the pay was lousy. Mildred's largesse was an anomaly. Quakers were big on simplicity and doing without, extending that philosophy to their hired help, lest someone like Mr. Kruller be tempted by wealth and take up bad habits, such as cross-dressing.

Before long I was up to my ears in employment—pulling weeds, painting porches, washing cars, and clipping hedges. Every house had a hedge to clip. The common hedge shapes were the standard box cut, the pretentious rounded cut, and my personal favorite, though the most difficult shape to achieve, the rolling wave trim.

Mildred Harvey's hedge was a standard box cut, her being a Quaker, not given to extravagance. The hedge was a deep source of pride to her. For the first three years of my employment I was not permitted anywhere near it. As Mildred aged, the task became too burdensome and she turned it over to me, overseeing the operation from the shade of a maple tree. The hedge clippers were old, dull, and weighed about a hundred pounds. Mildred Harvey had forearms like Popeye from wielding the hedge clippers over the years.

"What we really need are electric hedge clippers," I said. "They have them at Baker's Hardware for twenty-five dollars."

By then, Mildred had softened on the motorized assistance issue and the two of us piled in her 1969 Buick

Skylark and drove the five blocks to Baker's Hardware. Had I known what a harrowing experience that short drive would be, I would have trailed her on my bicycle. Her vision was failing, her motor skills in decline. She didn't so much steer, as point her car in the general direction she wished to go, sideswiping cars, streetlamps, and the occasional pedestrian. Mildred was oblivious to the destruction left in her path, cheerfully providing color commentary on each house, its past occupants, and their scandals. She was customarily circumspect, but when seated behind the wheel of a car, another, much more colorful, personality emerged.

When we arrived at the hardware store, the only space available required parallel parking. Though I didn't have my driver's license, I knew that to be the most intricate of all parking maneuvers. I closed my eyes and tightened my sphincter. By ricocheting her Skylark between the two cars, bouncing off the front car into the other, a two-ton pinball, Mildred eventually settled her Buick into the parking slot.

She turned off the car. "Here we are!" she said brightly. She leaped from the car with a vigor I'd never witnessed and hurried into Baker's, pulling me along in her wake.

Les Worrell was standing behind the hardware counter. "Hello, Mildred Harvey," he said. He wasn't a Quaker, but was familiar with their customs. "How may I help you?"

"We're here to purchase some electric hedge clippers," she said.

Lester led the way to the back corner where the lawn care equipment was displayed and pointed to the electric hedge clippers, pride etched in his features. "They're really something," he said. "Just plug them in and go."

We studied the clippers carefully, Mildred Harvey and I, standing side by side, hefting each one, pretending to cut with it, getting the feel of it.

"I like the green one," she said finally. "I've always been partial to green."

"We've had a lot of luck with the green ones," Lester said.

"Green's my favorite color," I added.

Les reached up and pulled the hedge clippers down from the shelf. He rang it up, then carried it like a newborn child out to Mildred's car, placed it in her trunk, and wished us luck.

A new convert to mechanical gadgetry, Mildred was not well versed in its use and insisted on storing the new clippers in her kitchen, based on the premise that they resembled her electric knife. I clipped the hedge once a month. Mildred would plan it a week in advance, phoning me on a Monday to suggest we trim the hedge the following Saturday. I would arrive at her home around ten, after the dew had lifted. She would retrieve the clippers from her pantry while I carried her rocker down from the porch and sat it under the maple tree.

We would string out the electrical cord, snake it past her rocker, through the kitchen window, and plug it in next to her coffee pot, where it could be dislodged with a quick yank. Despite her enchantment with the electric hedge clippers, she lived in mortal fear I would sever the cord and electrocute myself. Or worse, that I would hit a patch of moist hedge, short out the clippers and be shocked to death. She would run her hand over the hedge, satisfy herself that it was dry, check the sky for an errant rain cloud, then settle back into her chair, one hand gripped around the cord, ready to pull it from the wall in the event of trouble, then yell at me to turn on the clippers.

Every now and then, I would twitch and flop about, pretending I was in the throes of electrical shock, that thousands of volts were coursing through my body. Mildred would yank the cord; the clippers would fall dead; I would lie still on the ground, then stagger to my feet, dazed but determined to finish the job. It was always good for a tip.

With the motorized assistance issue resolved, Mildred and I settled into a deep friendship. I would stop by her home each day after school to see if she needed me. When weather permitted, we would sit on her porch, discussing future projects and joint ventures.

One summer day she announced, "I'd like for us to clean the chicken coop."

Mildred had butchered her last chicken years before, but had never gotten around to cleaning the coop. I'd peered into it a time or two, enough to know it was piled high with chicken dung, as if the chickens had been mainlining Ex-Lax. Poop on the beams, poop on the windows and, Great God Almighty, poop on the ceiling! A white, calcified crust of chicken poop covered every square inch of the coop.

It took me two days to scoop the poop. Mildred sat in her rocking chair underneath the maple tree urging me on.

On the third day, I woke up coughing and hacking, blowing great gobs of chicken-white mucus into my handkerchief. My eyes were matted with chicken crud, my brain mad with a histoplasmatic fever. I could barely raise myself out of bed. By nighttime I was delirious and giving serious thought to dying. I probably would have expired, except that Mildred Harvey learned of my predicament, fried up a chicken—the antidote to a virus being its inert form—waddled down to our home and stood over me while I consumed the entire chicken. The next morning I was revived, and that afternoon returned to Mildred's to report for duty.

"I think today we'll clean the barn," she said. I was growing weary of her inclusive pronouns since I was the one doing all the work. But I carried her rocker out to the barn and began pulling out one artifact after another, piling them on the lawn. There were cobweb threads everywhere, swaying slightly in the breeze, the musty sweetness of bygone manure lying gently upon the place.

Mildred recited the history of each relic as I drug it from the barn. Apple crates from when they'd grown apples in their backyard orchard. A worn saddle—her father's—now cracked and dry-rotted. The fireplace mantle from her grandparents' farmhouse west of town. It wasn't a barn cleaning as much as it was a thumbing through the family photo album.

"That old porch swing used to be on my parents' porch. Amos proposed to me when we were sitting on it." Mildred twisted her wedding ring on her finger, studying it.

Sitting by the barn that day, Mildred told me how she and her husband had met, how he'd worked at the bank, how they'd walked to the Quaker meetinghouse on Sabbath mornings with their children. I would meet Amos the next winter, when our youth group went to the nursing home on the highway outside of town to sing Christmas carols.

He was in the nursing home the whole time I worked for Mildred Harvey. He passed after I moved away. I came back to attend his calling at Baker's Funeral Home. Amos was reclining in the casket, Mildred was seated in a chair beside him. They each seemed relieved, as if they'd just arrived home from a long, grueling trip, which, in a way, I suppose they had.

Chapter 17

The Faith of My Father

In addition to bug spray, my father had other passions, most notably his unswerving devotion to the Weber grill, which eventually took on religious dimensions.

"Best grill ever made," he told me when I so much as glanced in the grill's direction. "They oughta give the guy who invented it the Nobel Prize."

Dad acquired his first Weber by trading three cases of bug spray for it. He barbecued steaks on the grill every Saturday night, with no regard for the weather. Two feet of snow could cover the land, the wind howling from the north at gale force, and my father could be found standing beside his Weber, whistling cheerfully and turning steaks.

The first Saturday of each month he and I would drive to Kroger, proceed to the charcoal aisle, and load bags of Kingsford into our cart, more than was sufficient for our needs, but my father was a Kingsford evangelist, distributing it among our neighbors and friends.

"What about lighter fluid?" I would ask.

He would look at me, shocked that any son of his would stoop to such sacrilege.

"No fluid of any sort! It ruins the flavor." He was death on gas grills for the same reason. Gas grills were an indication of moral laxity according to my father. A genial sort, he took most differences in stride and seldom held a grudge. But if anyone within earshot began extolling the virtues of gas grills, my father would load his verbal gun and blast away.

"I'd sooner eat raw meat than cook it on a gas grill," he'd say. "I'd rather die of trichinosis than eat that cancerous slop. There oughta be a law against it."

When my uncle Larry bought a gas grill, my father drove thirty miles into the city and pleaded with him to sell it. "You're killing your family," he told him. "Think of your children."

Dad preached the merits of the Weber grill with a fervor normally reserved for religion, buttonholing total strangers to boast of its qualities. He would visit Baker's Hardware Store and stand next to the Weber grill display, waylaying passersby, asking for a moment of their time to discuss their grilling future.

Yes, my father was a Weberite, and his high holy day Thanksgiving. He would awaken at five AM and begin sorting through a bag of Kingsford to select the prime briquettes. He would light the fire early, bringing the coals to a low, red heat, liberally sprinkling hickory woodchips on the embers.

"It's all in the hickory wood," he told me. "And not just any hickory wood. It's got to be from a tree at least a hundred years old, growing on a south-facing slope."

He had found just such a tree, but had kept its location a secret, a Weber apostle secreting away his Holy Grail.

But long before the fire had been lit, the turkey had been prepared with a priestly devotion. My father had several doctrines about turkey grilling that he adhered to without deviation, basting the bird with a mysterious concoction the day before Thanksgiving, rubbing its pink carcass with exotic spices, then laying his hands on it, beseeching the Lord to watch over it.

He took the turkey's weight, which he recorded on the wall inside our barn, along with the date, cooking times, and atmospheric conditions. *November 27, 1975, 23 lbs, start 6:59, end 12:37, barometric pressure 29.5 and holding, weather dry, turkey moist.*

He cooked the turkey slowly, with never more than twenty briquettes in the Weber, supplementing them from a bucket of spare coals, every now and then misting them down to prevent flare-ups.

He would carry the turkey into the house like a priest bearing the Eucharist, then trim it with a knife he'd sharpened on a whetstone the night before.

"A lot of people," he would say, slicing into the turkey with a surgeon-like precision, "use an electric knife. Bad mistake. That machinery taste bleeds right into the meat."

The turkey cut, my father would bear it to the table. We would bow our heads, and my mother would offer a Catholic prayer. "Bless us, O Lord, and these Thy gifts, which we are about to receive from Thy bounty, through Christ our Lord. Amen."

The Catholic prayer was a compromise. My parents were not given to table blessings, but the relatives who joined us for Thanksgiving were big on prayer, offering lengthy supplications over the turkey. They were Baptists and believed prayer should be spontaneous and from the heart, an opportunity to demonstrate their passion for the Lord. They would punctuate every sentence with the word *just*. "Lord, we just want to thank you Lord for just being there for us and just loving us and just caring for us the way you do. And Lord, we just ask you to just bless this food and just use it to strengthen our bodies so we can just serve you. And Lord, we just thank you for your son Jesus and for what he did for us, and we just thank you for your Word. Lord, we just love you and just want to make you happy and we just can't wait until you just come back here in your glory and take us all to heaven . . ."

By the time the praying wound to end, the gravy had scummed over and the mashed potatoes were cold lumps.

My Catholic mother could have the food blessed and the gravy circulating around the table within fifteen seconds, which distressed one of my more zealous cousins, who would add an altar call to my mother's prayer. "And Lord, while we have your attention, we just want to thank you for this cranberry sauce, which is red, reminding us of the blood you shed for us on the cross to pardon our sins if we'll just accept you as our personal Lord and Savior . . ."

No sooner would the prayer end than my father would begin his lamentation, apologizing for the turkey, which, though exquisite, never seemed to meet his strict criteria. One year it was too dry, the next year too moist. One year undercooked, the next year overcooked. One year over-seasoned, the next year bland. He would take a bite, spit the turkey into his napkin with a guttural *hauk!*, pronounce it unfit for human consumption, then lift the platter of turkey from the table so he could feed it to the dogs, not stopping until we'd assured him the turkey was fine, that it was the best he'd ever cooked.

The problem with grilling as your religion is that nothing ever reaches divine perfection, though my father's turkey came close.

Like any denomination, we Weberites had our favorite pews. The adults ate at the fancy table in the dining room, in the lap of Thanksgiving luxury. My brother David, who had something of a reputation for holiday decoration, had adorned the table with autumn ornaments—leaves, gourds, and small pumpkins. We children ate in the kitchen at a card table dubbed the no-frills table, promoted to the adult table only when an adult relative died and a vacancy opened.*

Nevertheless, that Weberite turkey had the power to transform even the humble circumstances of that card table in the kitchen, scrunched between the refrigerator and the stove.

It was, and we knew it, a holy moment when my father would carry that golden turkey in from the barn, steam rising in the November air.

"I don't know, I might have overcooked it this year. It might be too dry," my father would say, even as the bird glistened with juices.

I would close my eyes, willing that moment to last forever, the scent of turkey rising around me, the excited chatter of my family, my cousin trying to pray us into heaven, not realizing we were already there.

* I ate at the no-frills table until I was forty-five and my aunt Glenda passed away. The next year my parents moved to a house with a smaller dining room table and I was back at the no-frills table. People don't die fast enough in my family.

Chapter 18

Bill and Bunny

My father was the only bug spray salesman in town, indeed only one of three in the entire state, which gave the job a certain panache. Tim Hadley's dad was a school janitor, a noteworthy job, since it allowed us access to the Coke machine in the basement workshop. Peanut's father lived up in the city, working a mysterious job no one knew anything about, not even Peanut. Bill Eddy's dad was a school guidance counselor, but on nights and weekends made wooden doodads, which he sold at craft fairs across Indiana.

Like all fathers everywhere, they tended to be grouchy, except for Ralph Hadley, who went about his custodial duties with unwavering cheerfulness. During the flu season, with six to eight vomitings per hour, Mr. Hadley could be seen patrolling the school hallway, a mop in one hand, a bag of sawdust in the other, whistling contentedly. There was no shaking the man.

George Eddy churned out wooden puzzles, clocks, checker sets, letters, numbers, and other knickknacks by the thousands, which he and his wife, Libby, loaded into their Ford Esquire station wagon each Friday evening. Bill and I would watch from a hidden vantage point, lest we be drafted into helping.

"Where you going tomorrow?" I would ask in a whisper.

"To the Cornbread Festival," Bill would whisper back. "Want to come?"

"Sure, I like cornbread."

On any given Saturday, in any given direction, there were dozens of festivals or craft fairs to choose from—the Covered Bridge Festival in Mansfield, the Popcorn Festival of Clay County, the Navy Bean Festival in Rising Sun, the Elwood Chili Cookoff, or the Ligonier Marshmallow Festival. There were, and still are, more festivals in Indiana than in all the other states combined—annual celebrations of little-known foods, persons, plants, or architectural features, pageants honoring industries that had died years before—and the Eddys sold wooden doohickeys at every one of them.

The night before the festivals, I'd sleep on the floor beside Bill's bed, then wake up early the next morning to watch Libby Eddy cook bacon in the microwave oven. The Eddys owned the first microwave oven in our town, and

Libby was accustomed to an audience. The microwave was big, clunky, and emitted huge amounts of radioactive power, shorting out every pacemaker in a ten-mile radius, but it did a great job with bacon.

After breakfast, we would pile in the Esquire, Mr. and Mrs. Eddy in the front seat, Bill and me sprawled out atop the knickknacks in the back. One year, Mr. Eddy made nothing but letters, his Esquire filled with A's and P's and even Q's and Z's.

"Can't forget the Z's," he told me. "Especially if it's a sausage festival. Then you get your Poles and they all have Z's in their names—Zielinskis, Zuranskis, Zukowskas, Zawadzkis. One time I sold twelve Z's to a man named Zeztzl."

"What if," I asked Bill on our way to the Marshall County Blueberry Festival, "we had a wreck and I was thrown from the car and the letters D-E-A-D landed on top of me?"

"More likely the letters P-E-R-V-E-R-T would land on you," he said.

Bill Eddy was a laugh a minute.

After an hour in the car, lying on the letters, we would arrive at the festival, vowels and consonants pressed into our backs and butts.

Of all the festivals, my favorite was the Covered Bridge Festival in Mansfield, situated on the banks of Raccoon Creek. Bill had a canoe that Mr. Eddy lashed to the top of the Esquire, so we spent the day canoeing several miles upstream, then floating back down, coming to shore near an old mill that had recently been restored. The mill had been built in the mid-1820s. It had ceased operations in 1968, but several old men were on hand to give tours. They would start their memorized spiel, reciting the dramatic history of corn and its many virtues. Bill and I would interrupt when they paused to catch their breath, asking them corn questions: How much corn does there have to be in a corndog for it to be a corndog? Are there wheatdogs? Why do they call thick skin on your toe a corn? As corn fans, does it bother you to see something so unpleasant named after your favorite crop? If a cornucopia is shaped like a horn, why isn't it called a hornucopia? Had the corn people paid for naming rights? The corn men offered no satisfactory answers.

In late afternoon, we'd reload the Esquire and head back to Danville, Bill and me stretched out in the back, planning the rest of our weekend.

"How about we go camping?" he'd suggest.

Bill lived across the road from Mrs. Blanton's woods. Her house sat a quarter mile toward town, so it was a simple matter to slip into her woods unseen and spend the night, camping on the bluff above the White Lick Creek. We would arrive at the campsite just before dark, and set up camp. Since the woods were across from Bill's house, he was our de facto leader and would sit by the fire issuing orders. I would scurry about like Hop Sing on *Bonanza*, cutting firewood, cooking supper, toting water, pitching the tent, digging a pit toilet, then gathering soft pine needles for Bill to sleep on.

Bill was never one to do anything halfway, and he'd accumulated enough camping gear to equip an army—knives, hatchets, tents, stoves, cooking supplies, lanterns, backpacks, and sleeping bags. Before long, he had me loaded down like a pack mule, and though it was only a quarter mile from his home to our campsite, I was reduced to crawling the last hundred yards, dragging his equipment behind me. He would surge ahead, his hand shading his eyes, staring off into the distance, pointing to the horizon, urging me forward.

Occasionally, others would join our ventures. Don Dodson was a favorite companion, a consistent source of entertainment. The part of his brain responsible for self-restraint not yet developed, Don could always be counted upon to do something reckless for our enjoyment, usually involving hatchets, rifles, or other implements of death. In one of his more inspired moments, he placed me against a tree, counted off one hundred yards and fired at me with his .22 rifle to see how close he could come without hitting me. It was that kind of innocent fun that made my teenage years such happy ones.

We would sit by the campfire late into the night, me collapsed on the ground dog-tired, Bill resting against a nearby tree smoking a cigar.

"What you gonna do when we graduate?" he'd ask.

"Forest ranger," I'd say. "What about you?"

He would draw deeply on his cigar, look thoughtful, then say, "Plumber."*

---

* Bill did become a plumber, a very good one, and is now the most popular man in our town. I became a minister and haven't been invited to a party in years.

Whatever he undertook, Bill had a knack for landing on soft ground. His first job in high school was for the Walt Land Construction Company, where he was given *his own truck to drive!* This, at a time when driving any vehicle required weeks of negotiation with your parents, promising them you'd buckle down in school, attend church, and be nice to your sister. Even then, the car mileage was allotted like precious gems. "It's one mile to the grocery store," my mother would tell my brothers, checking the odometer on our car. "I don't want to see a tenth of a mile over two miles."

But on Bill's first day of work, Walt Land tossed him a truck key, twenty dollars, and said, "You drive that pickup. Let me know when you need more gas money." It was like giving a drug addict a bushel basket of cocaine. Bill nearly fainted dead away, and for the next two years could be seen driving the truck all over the western half of Indiana, running errands for Walt Land, always taking the long way around, driving south to go north, looping miles out of his way past our homes, where he'd bump the horn and wave.

Bill's teenage years possessed a magical quality. He had only to say aloud that he wanted something and it was as if an incantation had been chanted. Within a few hours he would possess it—a new bicycle, a new BB gun, a new pocketknife, a date with a certain girl. How he acquired these treasures, I do not know. His parents didn't give him the money, he never stole anything, he just had immense good luck. If a billionaire were ever spontaneously moved to slip a kid a thousand-dollar bill, Bill would have been the kid walking past at the exact moment of inspiration.

Bill had a mystical hold on me, and I was always endeavoring to stay on his good side. We'd ride our bicycles to the Dairy Queen, and I would plead with him to let me buy. He'd pause, mulling over my offer, then say, "Well, all right, if you really want to." I would order a cup of water for myself so I could spend more money on Bill. When we were delivering newspapers, I would beg to deliver his papers, happily adding his thirty-five customers to my twenty-six, and paying him for the privilege. He had such charisma he would have made a tremendous diplomat. Fortunately, he was good natured and never used his magnetism for immoral ends. Even now, people phone Bill daily, vying for his plumberly attention, pleading with him to drop by their house for a few moments to repair a clogged or leaky pipe, pledging to shower him with riches for his slightest consideration. It is unlike anything I have ever seen.

Bill knew everyone in town, and everyone knew him. Precocious didn't begin to describe him. I met him in first grade, and even then he was a man about town. Adults, when passing him on the street, would call out greetings, going out of their way to shake his hand or pat his head. It was like growing up best friends with Ronald Reagan. You were in the company of greatness, you knew it, and did everything within your power to remain in a position of favor. If Bill had asked me to kill someone, I would have looked him in the eye and asked, "Poison, knife, or gun?"

One of our associates was Bunny Runyan, whom we'd met delivering the *Great Hoosier Daily.* This was in the era of nicknames, when kids, as a matter of course, assigned alternative names to their peers, usually based on some physical peculiarity. My town was populated by children named Bucky, Gimps, Fats, Pizza Face, Crack, Carrot Top, Onion, and Dog Breath. Brad Runyan, Bunny's older brother, was nicknamed Rabbit, so it followed that Bunny would be Bunny.

Bunny Runyan, for as long as we were kids, was the picture of sunny optimism. We could be fifty miles from home on our bicycles with flat tires, our legs broken, tornadoes swirling about us, and Bunny would find the upside in it. But more than that, if there was even the faintest glimmer of good in a situation, Bunny would find it. "Boy, it sure is nice having that tornado at our backs. It's pushing us right along! Aren't we lucky!"

Bill, Bunny, and I spent many afternoons tromping through the woods outside of town, bristling with weapons, intent on killing any animal unfortunate enough to cross our paths. We were hampered by our poor eyesight, and our secret inclination toward pacifism. We liked the manliness of hunting, but the idea of spilling blood was repulsive to us, so we aimed wide, then blamed the miss on faulty equipment. For years, our campfire talks had to do with animals we'd almost killed and fish we'd almost caught.

In our later teenage years, we would take bicycle rides through southern Indiana, three or four days in length, letting only our moods determine the duration. Bunny had an abundance of relatives dispersed throughout the state. We would ride from one relative's home to another, sleeping on their fold-out couches. They all looked like Bunny and shared his traits of wild optimism and good humor. Some of the relatives were quite distant—third, fourth, and fifth cousins—but we were always warmly received. We had only to show up on their doorstep, announce our kinship, and we'd be welcomed into their home. One night, south of Terre Haute, Indiana, ninety miles from home, Bunny woke me in the middle of the night to tell me he'd just remembered his cousins had moved the year before.

"Then whose house are we sleeping in?" I asked.

"Not exactly sure," Bunny said. "But they sure are nice!"

We woke four hours later, ate bacon and eggs prepared by our hosts, said our good-byes, with Bunny's assurance that he would see them at the next family reunion.

The next day, we rode through the southern Indiana town of Loogootee, where a reporter, in search of news on a slow summer day, took our picture and wrote a story about us, supplemented with my liberal embellishment of our feats. Then we pedaled on to Paoli and stopped for lunch at Kaelin's Restaurant, where my future wife was waiting tables, saving for college, though I didn't know that then, or I'd have left her a tip.

After lunch, we rested in the shade of a tree on the courthouse lawn. "I was in this town once," Bill said. "Countdown to Christmas Festival. Year before last. Sold lots of Q's. Qualkenbushes, Qualls, Quinns. This town is full of Q's."

"I could be happy in a town with lots of Q's," Bunny said.

"There's nothing like a Q," I said agreeably. "I'm descended from a Q myself. Quinetts from Vincennes."

"That would be the Hedgehog Huzzah Festival," Bill said.

"Imagine that, a tribute to the lowly hedgehog," Bunny said. "What a great state we live in!"

Yes, indeed, what a state!

Chapter 19

Government Work

In the spring of my sixteenth year, Mr. O'Brien, our high school's guidance counselor, posted an advertisement on the bulletin board outside his office, urging teenagers to enlist in the Youth Conservation Corps, a program begun by the federal government to provide, in the words of its brochure, "meaningful employment to young people." I filled out an application, wrote the requisite three-page essay about why I wanted to work long hours for little pay, and mailed everything to Washington, D.C. Mr. O'Brien told me not to get my hopes up, that never in the history of the program had a kid from our town been selected to be part of the Corps. This was typical of Mr. O'Brien. His standard response to our aspirations was to tell us they were impossible, that we aimed too high, that we should give serious thought to pumping gas at Logan's Mobil. It was pure genius on his part, motivating us to prove him wrong.

Several months passed, and I'd forgotten I'd applied. Then I received a phone call telling me I'd been accepted and to report the next week at the Indiana Dunes National Lakeshore in Chesterton, Indiana, for an eight-week camp. "Twenty boys and twenty girls have been selected," the man told me. *Twenty girls!*

My parents seemed especially happy for my good fortune. Indeed, they seemed positively gleeful at my moving 150 miles away for the summer.

Peanut was beside himself with envy. "You're going to spend the summer away from home with twenty teenage girls?"

"It appears so," I said, neglecting to mention the other nineteen boys. "From what I understand, we'll be sharing living quarters."

I arrived at the camp on a Sunday afternoon and was assigned to a barracks with the other boys, across the camp from the girls, who were surrounded by land mines, razor wire, and armed sentries to discourage intermingling.

The camp director, a Mr. Neil Fleck, gathered us on the lawn for a pep talk. We would be paid fifty dollars a week, plus room and board, for the pleasure of "meaningful employment," mostly working nine hours a day picking up dead fish from the beaches of Lake Michigan. "You'll get a nice tan," he said, "and be doing your country a real service." For the entire eight weeks of camp, Neil Fleck appealed to our patriotism whenever our zeal for picking up dead fish dimmed.

The fish were called alewives. An Atlantic coastal fish, they'd invaded the Great Lakes during the 1950s and '60s, and were still mating like rabbits in 1977 when I was hired to clean them from the beaches. By some quirk of nature, millions of young alewives died during the summer months and washed up on the southern shore of Lake Michigan, where they were raked into great piles and buried by easily duped teenagers earning $7.14 a day.

It was a grotesque job, made worse by the camp cook who sent us off to work each morning with tuna fish sandwiches for lunch. Maggots swarmed over the dead alewives, and great clouds of flies rose from their rotted corpses. It was like one of the deeper levels in Dante's *Inferno*, and I spent the summer wondering what I had done to so deeply offend God that my life had come to this. I could think of several things, most of them having to do with impure thoughts.

Raking up dead fish with twenty girls was mindless labor, giving me more time to spend on impure thoughts. So strong was my libido that not even the stench of rotting fish could turn me from the path of romance. I had never had a girlfriend, but I reasoned that there being an equal number of boys and girls, the odds were even that by the end of summer I'd hit the jackpot. Unfortunately, the general consensus among the girls was that they loved me like a brother, thought of me as a dear friend, and didn't want to risk our relationship by engaging in any activity that might lead to hurt feelings. Even when I told them I was ready to assume that risk, they remained unswervingly devoted to preserving our friendship. Meanwhile, every spare moment found them out in the woods with the other nineteen boys, whom they apparently didn't love like brothers, while I stayed back at camp peeling potatoes. The entire camp was one surging hormone. Our counselors were college students, who quickly paired off and also spent much time in the woods, ostensibly studying nature.

The alewives were dying faster than we could bury them, so a fellow group of YCCers from another camp came to help for a week. This group was comprised mostly of girls, and their first day there I fell in love with one, and remarkably, she with me. We met at the beach. Her rake was clogged with dead, stiff alewives.

"Let me help you with that," I said, deftly plucking the alewives from the tines of her rake.

We worked side-by-side the rest of the morning, stopping occasionally to de-fish our rakes and smile longingly at one another. By lunchtime, we were in love, and I shared my tuna sandwich with her. That evening we went for a walk in the woods, then smooched behind the camp kitchen until our lips were chapped. When we parted a week later, she gave me her picture and promised to love me forever, forever lasting approximately one month, before she wrote to tell me she thought of me as a brother and wanted to be my friend. My lips had scarcely healed, and I was alone again. Naturally.

Midway through the summer, the assault of the alewives tapered off and we began building a trail through a nearby bog. Like much employment involving the federal government, it was obvious make-work, building a trail no persons in their right minds would ever hike. As a child I enjoyed watching war movies, and the trail building we did that summer was eerily reminiscent of the WWII movie, *Back to Bataan.* Each day we hacked our way through dense undergrowth, mosquitoes and horseflies tearing chunks of flesh from our gaunt, malarial bodies. We would stagger forward, on the verge of collapse, only to have Neil Fleck spur us onward, urging us to remember Valley Forge, the Alamo, the *Maine.*

Two weeks before camp was over, Neil Fleck announced we'd be driving to Kentucky where we would carry fifty pound backpacks thirty-five miles through the Appalachian wilderness and sleep on the ground. Everyone else was elated, but I sensed four days in the woods did not bode well for me or my spastic colon, and asked Neil Fleck to drop me off at a Holiday Inn and pick me up on their way back home.

"Nonsense! You'll love it!" he said, clapping me on the back. "It's a great American adventure! Think of Lewis and Clark! Think of Daniel Boone!" I was a dab under six feet tall and weighed 105 pounds. When the backpack was strapped to my body, my knees snapped, I collapsed in a heap, and thought of dying.

The next four days were so wretched I began to miss the alewives. Though I did not think it geographically possible, the entire thirty-five miles were uphill. It was the first week of August and egg-frying hot. On our way up the mountain, we passed camels who'd died along the trail. I drank all my water the first day and was reduced to sucking moisture from leaves I later learned were poison sumac.

On the second day, I fell behind the group, came to a fork in the trail and, consistent with my life's experience, took the wrong path. Within a few hours the trail petered out, and I stumbled into a clearing, hopelessly lost. Oddly, I felt quite cheerful, sensing the end was near, that I would soon be dead, my misery brought to a close. I had packed two pounds of M&M's in anticipation of this very scenario, telling myself that gorging on chocolate would ease an otherwise painful death. I was propped against a tree, halfway through the second pound of M&M's and fast descending into a sugary coma, when I heard Neil Fleck call my name. I was deeply annoyed. There were twenty miles left to hike and I was hoping to die in that sylvan glade, the beasts of the field in attendance, waiting for me to expire so they could eat me.

Instead, Neil Fleck placed his canteen to my sumac-poisoned lips, wiped my forehead with his handkerchief, eventually helped me to my feet, and escorted me back to the others, who clapped when they saw me, the boys slapping me on the back and the girls hugging me, in a sisterly sort of way.

The rest of the day was an exquisite joy, with two girls, one on either side of me, helping me along. After a few hours I was recovered, but kept silent about my improvement, enjoying the girls' close proximity. I moaned occasionally and let my eyes roll back so as to appear delirious, mumbling incoherently. Later, around the campfire I regaled my guardian angels with stories of my four-hour absence, slightly exaggerating the perils I had faced. "Timber rattlers as thick as my leg," I told them. "Falling out of trees and landing on my head."

One of the girls was Julianne, who, when I had asked her for a date the week before, had told me she was thinking of becoming a nun. But my brush with danger had apparently caused thoughts of celibacy to flee her mind. She scooted closer to me. "That must have been horrible," she said, laying her hand atop mine.

"I'd rather not talk about it," I said, leaning into her, settling my head against her generous Catholic bosom. "If you don't mind, I think I'll rest."

Julianne and I shared the last of my M&M's that evening. I gave her the green ones, which Peanut had told me were an aphrodisiac, but they had a soporific effect on her and she went to sleep. When she awoke the next morning she had committed herself anew to chastity and thought of me once again as a brother.

The last day of our hike it rained buckets, great sheets of water pouring over us. I was the last one in the van and for eleven hours was squeezed beside Neil Fleck, who sang the whole way home from a book of patriotic songs, pausing occasionally to point out a natural wonder or a strip mall. "Would you look at that! What a great country this is!"

Great, indeed.

The last day of camp we were driven to a hotel in Gary, Indiana—not yet the murder capital of the nation but well on its way—where we ate chicken in cream gravy and hard green beans. Neil Fleck gave a speech urging us to dedicate ourselves to the nation's betterment, and Julianne talked about how she loved each of us, then she began to cry, and just so she wouldn't feel bad, we cried with her, weeping that the summer had come to an end, pledging to remain dear friends for as long as we lived.

Chapter 20

My Grocery Days

Some of the first white people to settle in Danville were Quakers, who in obedience to the Scriptures were fruitful and multiplied. They worshipped in homes initially, but by the time my family arrived in 1957, had multiplied themselves into a handsome brick meetinghouse two blocks southwest of the courthouse. In defiance of Quaker custom, they'd added a steeple and bell, which was tolled every Sunday morning by a man we called Bambi, who was what people back then called slow. According to Peanut, Bambi's mother and father were brother and sister. I later learned that wasn't true, but Peanut spoke with such authority I believed it for years.

Bambi had cobbled together a patchwork of jobs. On Friday and Saturday nights he ushered at the Royal Theater, patrolling the dark rows, cooling the ardor of more passionate theatergoers, and cracking boisterous patrons on the kneecap with his Ray-O-Vac flashlight. On Sunday mornings, at precisely 10:25 AM, he entered the bell tower of the meetinghouse, seized the bell rope, and rang the bell three times—once for the Father, once for the Son, and once for the Holy Ghost. At least that was the stated purpose for ringing it three times. The real reason is that half the Quakers were deaf. After the first toll, they looked at one another, puzzled, and said, "What was that?" When the bell sounded again, they asked, "Do you mean that?" After the third strike, they said, "I think it's the bell. It must be time for church to start."

The meetinghouse was five blocks up Broadway from our house, so I could hear the bell calling the town's sinners to worship. I would glance at the clock over the television to make sure it was keeping time, then settle in to watch the Reverend Ernest Angley, live from the Ernest Angley Grace Cathedral in Akron, Ohio. Ernest Angley spoke in a nasal monotone and sported a wig that lay on his head like a piece of plastic. He worked miracles right and left—reconstructing ear canals, opening clogged arteries, restoring damaged nerves, regenerating severed limbs as if people were lizards and could sprout new appendages. As fascinating as the miracles were, it was the wig that grabbed my attention. It was cemented to Ernest's head, never moving, never graying, not one fake hair out of place, the thick, lush mane of a teenager at the peak of hair production, attached to Ernest Angley's liver-spotted head.

I watched Ernest Angley every Sunday morning for two years, mesmerized. Then I practiced faith healing with my brother Doug, each of us curing the other of various maladies. Watching Ernest Angley was infinitely superior to anything in the Catholic Church, and a habit I intend to return to in my final years, when I am most in need of a miracle, of having an aorta unclogged or my hearing restored.

When I was sixteen, an event occurred that altered the course of my life. My Quaker neighbors, the Comers, volunteered to lead their church's youth group. One Sunday evening, I watched from my porch as carloads of Quaker girls descended on their home, and I felt the Lord urging me toward the Quakers. So I forsook the Reverend Ernest Angley and for the next three years attended the Danville Friends Meeting, where I was often the only male in the youth group. Wanting to keep the odds in my favor, I never invited any of my friends to attend, despite the Comers' urgings to go forth into all the world and make disciples.

"Dreadful," was my typical response when asked by my friends how youth group was going. "I don't know why I attend." Then on Sunday evenings, I would recline happily in a beanbag chair in the Comers' living room, eating brownies, surrounded by Quaker girls, each of them cute as a pixie.

After a few evenings with the youth group, I began attending worship on Sunday mornings. The pastor of the

Quaker church was an eccentric, excitable man named Ed whose chief qualification for ministry was marrying the daughter of the search committee chairman. Ed had been raised Baptist, had no formal theological training, and was not constrained by that in any way. He was like a parrot dropped in among a flock of crows. I looked forward to Sunday mornings, to hearing what he would say from the pulpit. Carefully nuanced theology was not Pastor Ed's strong suit. But what he lacked in spiritual prowess, he made up in drama.

"Did you know," he thundered one Sunday morning, "that in the Bible, women of ill repute wore blue dresses! And that is true to this day!" He went on and on, a one-man committee against blue dresses.

I glanced down the row at a woman who that morning had selected from her modest Quaker wardrobe a bright blue dress. She was scrunched down, her head barely visible above the back of the pew. Her husband was patting her hand, his threadbare scalp turning red.

The pulpit emboldened Pastor Ed; outside of it, he was a lamb, a consummate politician, phoning the shut-ins each morning to make sure they hadn't died in their sleep. Whenever a whiff of rumor circulated about his being asked to move on, the Quaker widows would come to his rescue, hobbling into the meetinghouse on their walkers, determined to save him. So he stayed on, all through my high school years, charming some and infuriating others.

I liked Ed, mostly because of his ability to make an otherwise dull venture such as church interesting. Where once I had dreaded church, I looked forward to Pastor Ed's latest revelation. Each Sunday, he targeted a different adversary, another enemy of the Lord—blue-dressed women one week, Masons the next, and Catholics the week after that. I returned week after week, the Quaker hook setting deeper in my mouth, until I was reeled in and Pastor Ed landed me on the dock, displaying me to the gathered Quakers, proud of his catch, a Catholic boy saved from Romanism and brought into the Lord's True Church.

Quakers had a reputation for fair dealing and attracted a good number of the town's business people, one of whom was Orville Johnston. Orville and his wife, Esther, owned the IGA grocery store on the west edge of town, across from St. Mary's Catholic Church. Ours was a Kroger family, Kroger buying more bug spray from my father than IGA, but on Sunday mornings my mother would stop by the IGA after church to buy Saps doughnuts with rainbow sprinkles. The doughnuts were displayed in a revolving case, next to the lunch meat. The meat man would come out from behind the counter and count our doughnuts into a box. This imparted a meaty flavor to the doughnuts, which for years I assumed was their natural flavor.

I had inadvertently made a favorable impression on Orville Johnston, and one Sunday after church he asked me to drop by his store that week. He was circumspect, it being the Sabbath, an improper time to discuss the affairs of business. When I stopped by the next day, he summoned me into his office. It was early winter, well past Labor Day, but Orville was wearing white shoes, as if he had just stepped off *The Lawrence Welk show*. Esther was seated behind the desk, her glasses perched on the end of her nose, entering figures into a ledger.

The office was tiny, so Orville and I stood while he interviewed me, him pausing occasionally to wait on a customer.

"We need a stock boy," he said. "It's an important job. You're on the front line of customer service. You must always be polite to the customers, look your best, get along well with your coworkers, and work hard. Can you do that?"

I had serious doubts, but needed a job, so I nodded my head and stuck out my hand. "I'm your man," I said, shaking Orville's hand.

"When can you start?" Orville asked.

My father had told me Orville would ask this as a test of my willingness to work. "I've come prepared to work, sir," I said, feeling a bit like Eddie Haskell on *Leave It to Beaver.*

"Then the job's yours," Orville said, clapping me on the back. "You can start by racking bottles."

This was back in the days when pop came in glass bottles, which could be returned to the grocer for a nickel. This was a chief source of revenue for the children of my generation, a revenue stream with which I was well acquainted.

The bottles were stacked in the back room, next to the walk-in freezer. The empty bottles were arranged in rows according to their brand. The soda men came each week to collect the bottles, but it was startling how many bottles could accumulate in seven days. In any given week, the grocery store collected thousands of bottles, all of them gunky and sticky with the hardened dregs of soda congealed in the bottom. It was not uncommon to find a mouse set in the cola like an insect trapped in ancient amber.

Racking bottles was a spiteful task, one the other stock boys had became adept at avoiding. Esther would click the intercom button twice, then blow into the microphone. The other stock boys would scatter to the winds, knowing we were about to be summoned to rack bottles. They each had an escape route—Tony Lobbia would hurry out the front door to gather carts from the parking lot, Tim Spotila would flee to the bathroom, and Lance Oppy would seize the nearest jar of pickles, hurl it to the floor, then yell, "Cleanup on aisle three. I'll get it." This left Steve Dickey and me to rack the bottles, holding our breath, tossing cases of bottles into the room, the air thick with a sugary humidity, mice hurling themselves at the bottles to get at the soda.

Other than that, it was a grand job for a teenage boy. Orville was generous, paying fifty cents above minimum wage, and incurably cheerful, sallying through the store calling out encouragement to his employees. I once knocked over a display of sweet pickles, breaking dozens of jars, and Orville clapped me on the back, smiled, and said, "Could've been worse. Could've lopped off a finger on the meat saw." Orville lived in mortal fear that someone would fall into the saw and be dismembered, ending up in the hamburger. Whenever the saw kicked on, the lights would dim, Orville would flinch, listen for blood-curdling screams, then slowly relax when none came.

In addition to the meat saw, he also feared gypsies, regularly warning us to keep an eye out for them, lest they overrun us. I had never seen a gypsy except on *Bonanza*, when Little Joe fell in love with a gypsy girl. The *Bonanza* gypsies wore bright clothing, rode in horse-drawn wagons, played tambourines and guitars, sang a lot, and looked like Larry Storch on *F Troop*. I was reasonably certain I could pick one out in a crowd, but Orville wasn't so sure.

"They'll sweep in here a dozen at a time, rob you blind before you know it, then be gone like that," he said with a snap of his fingers.

Gypsies sounded fascinating to me, and for years I prayed for them to descend on us, but they never did. There was, however, a kleptomaniac who showed up every Friday at lunchtime. A well-liked woman in our town, she was fond of lunch meat, and would stuff her pockets with bologna, pimento loaf, and salami, then cruise past the potato chip aisle and stock up on Fritos. Orville would follow behind her discreetly, keeping track of her plunder, then present a bill to her husband. It never occurred to Orville to phone the police or make a scene, preferring to protect the woman's reputation and not embarrass her publicly. Orville was pure class.

Orville loved a good sale and was adept at luring customers to his store with the promise of a bargain. Several times a year he held an unlabeled can sale, piling hundreds of cans whose labels had fallen off in a large bin and selling them five for a dollar. My mother would stock up during these sales. For the next month our dinners would be a grand adventure, a stew of unmatched foods—chicken noodle soup and prunes with condensed milk and peanuts. The four basic food groups in one fell swoop!

But Orville was at his best on Mondays, when the delivery truck came out from the city to replenish the shelves. He was a grand conductor, with a pointed finger or arched eyebrow directing a case of fruit cocktail here, a box of cookies there, a harmonious symphony of food distribution and display. And the pickles! Pickles were everywhere, omnipresent. We sold more pickles than any IGA on God's green earth—dill, kosher dill, pickled dill, garlic dill, sweet, half sour, bread and butter, candied, three types of pickled pepper pickles, Polish pickles, German pickles, and gherkins, to name only a few. We had a twenty foot run of pickles, four shelves high. Pickle aficionados from across the nation came to view our pickle selection while Orville looked on with a deep pickle pride.

The pickle boxes alone yielded a mountain of cardboard, which was burned in the store's incinerator. Orville loathed the incinerator, fearing it would spark a conflagration that would level the west end of town. After Orville and Esther had left for the day, Tony Lobbia and I would stoke the incinerator to a red-hot heat, causing everything within twenty feet to spontaneously combust. We would rush toward the flames, hurling pickle boxes into the blaze, the heat singeing our eyebrows. In the wintertime, Tony and I would come in frozen from gathering the carts and stand before the incinerator, the heat washing over us in waves, us turning and roasting like the rotisserie chickens in the meat department. It boggles the mind to think a handful of teenage boys were left in charge of a building well-stocked with charcoal lighter, matches, and other incendiary devices, but that was a different era.

After a little while, Orville began wooing me toward a career in the grocery business, bringing his college textbooks from home, pressing them on me, promising an exciting career in food sales was mine for the asking.

My father warned me against it. "It doesn't pay well, and the hours are long," he said. "Don't do it."

So I became a minister instead.

I didn't tell Orville of my intended career change, hoping to string him along and get a promotion, maybe to head stock boy. But he gave that job to Tim Spotila. The rest of us, naturally, turned on Tim, accused him of being a suck-up, and left broken pickle jars for him to clean up.

Orville eventually sold the store, and I haven't had a decent pickle since. It's funny how life turns out. If I had kept my job with Orville, he might have sold the store to me and I'd have been the Pickle King of central Indiana, a not altogether unpleasant fate.

Chapter 21

Driving

My sixteenth fall I went to the Bureau of Motor Vehicles to take the test for my driver's license. Indiana being a one-party state, the BMV was under the firm control of the Republicans, who'd hired their extended families to manage the license branches, creating an atmosphere of entitlement and inefficiency. The bureau was administered like a banana republic, where privileges were extended or withheld by whim. I passed the test with flying colors, my father being a Republican, and began my search for suitable transportation.

Car selection was a tricky matter in those days. Automotive loyalties ran deep. Affordability wasn't the only factor in the equation. There were Ford families, Chevy families, AMC families, and Plymouth families. You had no choice in the matter. You were born into your brand, and switching from one to the other was not done lightly.

When my family washed up on the shores of Danville in 1957, we owned a Plymouth Belvedere, fondly referred to in family lore as the Batmobile. It was sky blue and aqua, sported tail fins a mile long, a formidable engine, and not one seat belt. My father would drive, my mother seated beside him, we five children strewn across the back seat, flung about like bowling pins whenever my father would brake or turn a corner.

While an aqua car seems unusual now, it was par for our course. My father actively sought out ugly cars, cars that had sat for long months on Nort Watson's car lot, cars so peculiar no one else wanted them. Orange, purple, and aqua cars Nort Watson sold to the desperate and blind. My father would settle his sights on a car, then spend months negotiating its purchase, hauling me to Nort Watson's, where we would listen to Nort extol the virtues of the AMC automobile.

"Now you keep an eye on these Gremlins," Nort would confide to my father. "They're gonna sell like hotcakes. There's not a finer car made today. Period."

Nort Watson ended every other sentence with the word *period*, a verbal exclamation point to hammer home his point.

Dad would wander over to the apple green AMC Pacer he'd been considering, standing back a dozen feet to admire it.

"You better get that car today," Nort Watson would say. "I had a man in just yesterday looking at it. Said he'd be back today to buy it."

It was a bald lie, and my father and I knew it. No one ever lined up to buy the kind of car my family would own.

Bad cars ran in our family. We were flops when it came to car selection and would, with unerring instinct, select the one automotive disaster from the hundreds of models available for purchase. Our family reunions were a veritable smorgasbord of failed transportation—Edsels, Vegas, Pintos, Corvairs, and Gremlins. One cousin had a Ford Pinto that had the amusing habit of bursting into flames at odd moments. Another cousin's Vega broke in half while he was crossing railroad tracks. That's right, broke in half, as in two separate but equal pieces. It was said of Vegas that they began rusting on the showroom floor. My family drove them in droves.

My grandfather Quinett owned a station wagon whose top was made almost entirely of glass, but because he was cheap he didn't have air-conditioning installed. He did, however, order power windows. A not-yet-perfected innovation, they soon failed with the windows in the raised position, leaving my grandfather with a terrarium on wheels. The sun baked the car's interior, water condensed on the inside, running in rivulets across the glass, dripping onto our heads. One August, I rode with my grandparents from Danville to Fond du Lac, Wisconsin. Seven hours on the broil setting. I arrived ten pounds lighter, basting in my own juices, mad with fever.

"Would you look at that blue sky!" my grandfather said every other mile, peering up through the glass roof. "What a car this is! You don't get views like this with just any car."

This was another family trait concerning automobile selection—we were so determined not to acknowledge our error that we would buy the same model of car over and over again, rather than admit we had made a mistake. Had they been available, I have no doubt my grandfather would have ordered glass-topped cars with broken windows for the rest of his life.

My father deviated from his usually cautious car-buying only once, with disastrous results. We were eating at the Dog N Suds Drive-In one Friday night when my father gazed across Main Street toward Dugan's Chevrolet and saw a brown Malibu, a red pennant tied to its antenna flapping seductively in the breeze. The spotlight hit the Malibu, the background music swelled, and my father swooned.

"Would you look at that!" he said. "What a car!"

He was nearing forty, with five children and two dogs, tilting hard against the windmills of middle age. As if in a trance, he opened our car door, walked across Main Street, straight toward the Malibu. An hour later, we were sporting new wheels.

My father loved that car, waxing it every Saturday under the tulip tree in our side yard. By then, his bug spray company made car wax and he became an evangelist for shiny cars. In the trunk of his car he carried tins of car wax, which he dispensed like a Baptist preacher passing out salvation tracts. He accosted total strangers on the street, pressing a can of car wax into their hands, urging them to polish their cars while there was yet time.

The Malibu glistened like a diamond, so deep was my father's love for it. He would sit in it for hours at a time, touching the steering wheel, rubbing his hands across the Naugahyde interior. On Saturday nights, my brother Doug and I would join Dad in the car, listening to the Indiana Pacers on the radio. Slick Leonard was their coach, our state's high priest of basketball.

One Saturday our family piled in the Malibu and drove forty miles west to Rockville, to Slick Leonard's basketball camp, and met the man himself. Slick was seated behind his desk, a tall man with long sideburns, wearing a plaid leisure suit, the picture of Hoosier success. After years of selling bug spray, my father could converse with anyone. Mimes had been known to break into senseless jabber around him, so gifted was my father in conversation. But he fell mute before the great Slick Leonard. Dad's mouth opened, but no sound emerged. We stood dumbly in front of Slick's desk, staring across at him, slack jawed, while he autographed pictures of himself, then walked us outside to our car. As we neared the Malibu, my father's spirit was revived and he found his voice.

"That's my new car," he said to Slick.

Slick Leonard studied the car, silently appraising it, then said, "I'm a Ford man myself."

The next day, my brother Doug drove the Malibu to the Dairy Queen and scraped it against a telephone pole, creasing the driver's door. When we got home and told Dad, he didn't even cuss. If it had happened the day before, he would have frothed at the mouth, but Slick Leonard had already taken off the shine. A few years later, my father sold the Malibu and bought an orangey-red Plymouth Horizon, another high-water mark of automotive design.

Given this history of vehicular disasters, it was no surprise that after passing my driving test I began driving a 1968 Volkswagen Beetle. It had belonged to my brother Glenn, who had joined the Coast Guard, sailed to Guam, and had written home to tell me I could have his car. This is a matter of some dispute. He claimed he gave me permission to drive it, while I was under the impression he'd given it to me. I forged his name on the title, sold it to Dugan's for five hundred dollars and, compounding my error, bought a 1974 Volkswagen Beetle.

Owning a Volkswagen Beetle in those days was akin to joining a cult in which all reality was suspended. The faithful were continually boasting of the Beetle's virtues, though keeping it running consumed all one's time, money, and effort. But only its merits, which were few, were ever spoken about. Beetles were notoriously unreliable, hazardous, bitterly cold in the winter, hot in the summer, and had a knack for breaking down at the worst possible time in the worst possible place. The Beetle was Hitler's brainchild, for God's sake, and assumed every nasty trait that man ever possessed, inflicting cruelty after cruelty upon its owners.

My Beetle repairman was Warren, who lived in the town north of us, though it would have been more convenient for all concerned if he had lived in our guest room, so frequent were our visitations. I began every day by driving the nine miles to his shop, knowing I would end up there eventually that day and wanting to save myself the trouble of having to guess when. He would labor underneath my Beetle, calling out encouragement, stoking the myth of Beetle superiority. "Yeah boy, they sure don't make them like this anymore. What a car!" After every repair, he would boast of the VW's mechanical soundness by saying, "Why, I wouldn't hesitate to drive it to California." I had no idea how people in California bragged about their cars.

Though the Volkswagen had many faults, its chief liability was an exhaust leak, which caused the passenger compartment to fill with noxious fumes. In the summer, this was remedied by lowering a window, but in the winter I couldn't drive very far without being overcome by carbon monoxide. I would find myself getting woozy, the Beetle would careen from shoulder to shoulder, oncoming cars would speed past in a honking blur. Eventually, I would lose consciousness, slow to a stop, and come around a few minutes later, the VW tilting into a ditch. The fog would lift, and I would resume my journey, undeterred. Had I been raised in a normal-car family, I would have been alarmed, but danger and mayhem seemed to me the natural course of things when men and cars got together, and I never gave it a second thought.

Chapter 22

The Blizzard

On January 25, 1978, a few weeks shy of my seventeenth birthday, a blizzard barged into Indiana, dumping twenty inches of snow on Danville. Temperatures dropped to below zero, and with wind gusts of fifty-five MPH, the wind chill hit –50°. The snow fell two days, the state was declared a disaster area, and every road in Indiana was closed. That this should happen so early in my life was providential, providing me the opportunity to say at every snow afterward, in a dismissive, old man voice, "Huh, you think this is bad, you should have seen the winter of '78!"

My father was on the road peddling bug spray, stranded in a hotel in Terre Haute, where he stayed five days and four nights, dining on filet mignon and shrimp cocktails, watching cable television, a rarity in those days, and whooping it up with other marooned salesmen. When the roads were finally opened, it took a crowbar to pry the salesmen from the place. My father phoned each night to report that he was still alive, his voice crackling and harassed over the wires, as if wolves were snarling outside his door. It took him twenty years to tell us about the filets and cable television.

We'd been sent home from school at noon, the first time our superintendent, Mr. Cox, had ever sent students home early. He was of the opinion that overcoming impossible odds was good for your character. I remember mushing my dog team through ten-foot drifts to get to school when every school in a three-state area had closed but ours.

Chick and Glenn had moved from home, which left my mother, my brothers David and Doug, and me to soldier on through the blizzard. I have forgotten how I spent our confinement, but suspect much of the time was passed fighting with my brothers, given our feral natures. Regular television programming had been suspended so the weatherman could tell us what we already knew, that the state was snowed in and no one was going anywhere. By the second day, matters had turned desperate. We were without heat and food, reduced to burning family heirlooms in our fireplace and eating a box of oyster crackers we'd discovered in the back reaches of the pantry.

Charley Williams, our chief of police, commandeered snowmobiles from Denny Grounds, who owned the Ford dealership. The policemen rode all about town delivering workers to the hospital, medicine to the sick, even transporting a dead body into town from out in the country. My mother called Charley to see if he could bring us milk, to no avail. We phoned in various emergencies—a possible ruptured appendix, a suspicious character wearing a face mask walking past our home, a car stuck in a snowdrift—suggesting that as long as Charley was coming our way, he might bring a gallon or two of milk, but he saw right through us.

For years, my mother had been after my father to wallpaper the kitchen, which the previous owners had painted a bright royal blue. She'd bought the wallpaper the previous summer and had stored it in the basement, where it had sat waiting for my father to be sufficiently motivated to hang it. He had never hung wallpaper and was hesitant about learning, knowing it would only lead to heightened expectations.

The third day of the blizzard, our next-door neighbors, Lee and Mary Lee Comer, came to check on our welfare. My mother greeted them at the door, wan and listless, faint with hunger, her fingers blackened with frostbite.

"Can we do anything for you?" Lee asked.

My mother brightened. "Do you know how to wallpaper?"

Mary Lee did the paste work, Lee hung the paper, and my brothers and I watched, enthralled. It was the first time we'd seen a home improvement project done without the accompaniment of fervent swearing.

Lee was masterful, a wallpaper virtuoso, cutting the wallpaper with mathematic perfection, butting up each piece of wallpaper to its neighbor, the pattern matching with a flowery precision. My mother was beside herself, in a full-blown state of elation, first gluing a section with Mary Lee, then helping Lee hoist a piece into place, an orchestral conductor, directing her personal *Ode to Joy*.

Eight hours later, the paste cleaned up and put away, the ladder stowed in the basement, we stood in the kitchen, marveling at the transformation.

"What do you think?" Lee asked.

"Now if we only had milk," my mother said.

The Comers came back the next day to play Monopoly and listen to the Statler Brothers on our bug tape player. I was, and remain, a notorious cheater when it comes to the game of Monopoly. I appointed myself treasurer, swiped five-hundred-dollar bills when no one was paying attention, and won the game, though the only properties I owned were Baltic Avenue and the Water Works. When my theft was discovered, I was jailed for five turns, but managed to oversee my criminal enterprises from my cell and came out richer than ever.

Midway through the day, word arrived at our home that the Kroger had reopened. The Kroger was a mile and a half from our house, the roads were still closed, and it was bitterly cold, but I volunteered to walk to the grocery store to get milk, wanting only to appear virtuous for volunteering, never dreaming my mother would actually let me go.

"Get some Oreos while you're there," she said. "And eggs too."

I didn't have winter boots, so I wore two pairs of socks and bread bags over my shoes. I pulled on long johns, then two pairs of pants, three shirts, an extra coat, and my father's Green Bay Packers hat. My little brother, David, circled around me, jackal-like, sensing vulnerability. "If you don't come back, can I have your bicycle?" he asked.

I had long dreamed of doing something heroic for my family, of killing an intruder with my bare hands, or some other dramatic display of bravery. Fetching milk hadn't occurred to me, though it would do, no other opportunities for valor having presented themselves.

It took an hour to reach the store, cutting through the woods to U.S. 36, which was still closed. There were a few snowmobiles out and about, policemen whizzing here and there, dozens of kids sledding on the hill behind the school. I pressed on, the bread bags leaking, my feet growing numb with cold. Down Main Street past the Phi Delts' clubhouse, which several men had succeeded in reopening and were lubricating themselves against the wintry chill. Up the hill, past the jail and the Waffle House, where more police snowmobiles were parked. I saw the officers inside, ghostlike through the steamy windows, eating doughnuts, a sight comforting in its familiarity.

The Kroger sat next to the Waffle House. The lights were on, and a few people were moving about inside. The manager—I won't mention his name because he is still alive and I'm still mad at him—met me at the front door to tell me they were closed.

"Closed? How can you be closed?" I asked. "It's the middle of the day. I see people buying groceries. All I need are milk, eggs, and Oreos."

I began to shiver, hoping to soften him, but he didn't budge from the doorway. "Nope. We're closed."

"The baby's puny," I told him. "The doctor said he needs milk or he'll die." There hadn't been a baby in our home in fifteen years, but my parents were Catholic, and I was banking on him thinking Catholics had either just had a baby or were making plans to have one.

"Come back tomorrow," he said, shutting the door in my face.

I beat on the glass window, tears and snot freezing on my face. "Powdered milk," I yelled. "How about powdered milk?"

Walking home was a misery. The wind cut down Main Street, knifing through my coat. I took a shortcut through the woods, crossed the creek and fell through the ice, the water poured into the bread bags. By the time I reached home, my feet were iced-up blocks. I propped them in front of the fireplace, warmed by the last remnants of heat generated from burning the family photo albums.

"The manager wouldn't let me in," I told my mother. "He said they were closed and for me to come back tomorrow."

My mother, normally a calm, unruffled sort, wove a rich tapestry of invective against the Kroger Corporation, starting with its president and working her way down to its lowliest stock boy, reserving her most colorful language for the local manager, a man who "by God, attended church with us and knew us and should act like the Christian he claims to be!"

If it is true that difficulties reveal a person's character, my father rose to the occasion. Serving at the time on the town board, in charge of the street department, he was seventy miles removed in his town's darkest hour. But he phoned the town workers each day, in between his steak dinners, urging them to greater heights, stirring their civic pride.

Unfortunately, my father's civic commitments had had a way of expanding my own obligations. Previous snowfalls had resulted in dozens of phone calls from widows whose driveways had been filled with mounds of snow left by the plows. I was assigned the task of digging them out, so they could go forth onto the ice and fall and break their hips.

The first time this happened, I came home with pocketfuls of money, which I showed my father. He frowned. "We do not take money from widows. I want you to give it back." There was no arguing with my father, this being in the olden days when children obeyed their parents, or else.

My father was often magnanimous at my expense, volunteering me for one unpleasant task after another, most of them having to do with dead animals, clogged toilets, or snow. Unlike him, I had no qualms about taking money from widows. I'd been mowing their yards for several years and had taken a considerable sum of money from them without hesitation. Snow, apparently, was different. God sent it to test our neighborliness, to remind us of our mutual dependence. Snow was not to be capitalized upon for personal gain. Or so my father's theory went.

But Dad backed me when it mattered. When he returned home on the fifth day after the blizzard, he drove promptly to the Kroger and told the manager to find a new supplier of bug spray, that he no longer wished to do business with a man who "by God, attended church with us and knew us and should act like the Christian he claims to be!"

When the town board elections were held the next year, my father ran on the good-neighbor platform, shaking every hand in town, passing out bug spray, working me like a borrowed mule from dawn to dusk, courting the widow vote. He was swept into office, appointed president of the town board, ably steering our town through its next great crisis—the Great Sewer Backup of 1981.

It no longer snows like it once did. But in those days before global warming, great storms would roll in from the northwest, burying our town. Men would die walking to the barn to feed the livestock. We would find them in the spring, ten feet from the back door. Still, those were good days, if you survived them, which most of us did, giving us something to talk about in our later years.

Chapter 23

Leaving Home

I graduated from high school in 1979, seated at graduation between Teri Griswold and Tim Hadley, my alphabetical compatriots since first grade. I was safely in the middle of the pack, grade-wise. Mike Fowler was our valedictorian and gave a speech about how we'd been the finest class to ever inhabit the halls of the Danville high school, that we were destined for greatness, that no obstacle was too high for us to overcome. I looked down the row at Jerry Sipes, seated between Bill Kirtley and Dee Kirts, not even bright enough to arrange himself alphabetically, and thought Mike Fowler was more optimistic than circumstances merited.

Our principal, Mr. Max Gibbs, shared Mike's high opinion of us, saying what an honor it had been to have us as students. He had done a remarkable job the past four years keeping his admiration a secret, but our class was in a charitable mood, willing to forgive and forget past animosities. Then he called our names, one by one, pausing for a moment before calling Jerry Sipes's name, weighing whether to confer a diploma, then decided the prospect of having Jerry for another year was too great a burden to bear, so called his name.

I had not distinguished myself and read my diploma several times before convincing myself it was authentic—no asterisks, no footnotes, no P.S. at the bottom noting the failing grade I'd received in geometry—just the usual high-sounding words, with my first name misspelled with two *l*'s, and Max Gibbs's signature across the bottom, a heavy dot of ink in the M, as if he'd hesitated to mull it over before signing.

Then, on cue, we turned the tassels on our caps from the right to the left, Father Roof from the Episcopal church prayed for our future—a tentative, wobbly prayer, every word underlined with doubt—then we marched from the gymnasium, up the hallway to the cafeteria, where Mrs. Blume yelled at Jerry Sipes one last time when he threw his mortarboard like a Frisbee. But even her screeching was tinged with an obvious affection for his zany antics, and when she cuffed him upside the head, it wasn't nearly as hard as she had done in the past.

My parents had invited the neighbors, Lee and Mary Lee Comer, over to the house for ice cream and cake, a round chocolate cake that had flopped in the heat, a fitting symbol of my tendency to collapse under pressure. I was presented with a suitcase, a subtle hint that it was time to leave home. My older siblings had gone to college, an undertaking I wished to avoid, hoping to put off further responsibilities as long as I could.

The next week I was hired by the local electric company to operate computers after passing a test that revealed, in stunning contradiction to my grades, an aptitude for math and logic. I was paid what was then a staggering sum, eight hundred dollars a month, which I burned through like a drunkard in a liquor store.

My father had wanted me to attend college and wasn't taking my resistance to higher education well. College brochures began appearing next to my placemat on the kitchen table, under my pillow, on the toilet tank. The slightest reference to a college—the first notes of the Notre Dame fight song, an IU ball game—would fire his boosters and send him into orbit. "I wish I had gone to college. I wish someone had offered to send me to college. I'd have done it in a heartbeat, I tell you that right now."

My father's own success was a strong argument against college. His bug spray job paid well, he'd been promoted into the furniture polish and car wax division, he was president of the town board, and we lived in one of the finer homes in town.

"You didn't go to college and you turned out all right," I pointed out.

"You think jobs like mine grow on trees," he said. "You think you can just go out and start selling bug spray today. Times have changed. You need college. Big Ed Danowski's son applied for a job at the company, and they told him to come back after college. Big Ed Danowski's son!"

Big Ed Danowski was a legend in the bug spray circles in which my father moved. This was sobering news.

When September came and my friends left for college, Dad's campaign to usher me into self-sufficiency increased. A wily negotiator, he took me out to dinner and gave a touching speech about how I'd become a man, a Protestant version Bar Mitzvah. "Of course," he said, skillfully segueing into part b of his talk, "with the privileges of adulthood come the responsibilities. Your mother and I have decided to charge you rent."

Two hundred dollars a month, not to put too fine a point on it, one-fourth of my income, plus four hours of yard work each Saturday.

In the end, it was the yard work that broke me. My dad had a tendency to overestimate my capacity for work, regularly assigning me Herculean tasks that a platoon of men couldn't have completed in a week's time. "First, I want you to mow the lawn (three acres with a push mower), then clean the gutters (the house was three stories high), and paint the barn," he announced over breakfast on a typical Saturday morning. This, he reasoned, should take no more than three hours, four at the most.

As the months passed, my duties expanded, the rent increased, and my father cut my rations. My free time was limited to a half hour each Sunday afternoon, in honor of the Sabbath. Rather than live in indentured servitude, I began plotting my escape, and on a Saturday afternoon, while my parents had gone to visit relatives, I struck off the shackles, packed my Volkswagen, and by way of an underground network established by sympathetic Quakers, fled to an apartment in the next town.*

I would eventually return to my parents' house to visit (the next day for Sunday dinner, in fact), but would never move back. I settled into an apartment owned by a mortician, and one summer day looked through the kitchen window and saw a lovely young lady, even lovelier than Miss Huddleston, walk by carrying a baseball mitt, a rather curious accessory.

I went outside and approached her. "Haven't I seen you somewhere before?" I asked smoothly.

She studied me closely. "Kaelin's Restaurant. Paoli, Indiana. You didn't leave a tip."

"I was saving my money to take you on a date," I said.

That weekend we went to a revolving restaurant on top of a hotel in Indianapolis where I left a big tip. Two years later we were married and eventually moved to Danville, and now have two sons who do the things I used to do, which worries me sick and makes my parents laugh.

* In retrospect, my depiction of those months might be exaggerated, but it seemed prison-like at the time.

Epilogue

My parents remained in the family home until the spring of 2005, when the challenges of aging necessitated a move. It was a transition I had urged them to make, not considering the effort it would take to empty, sort, disperse, organize, and clean seven thousand square feet of house, barn, and their contents. But eight dumpsters and a moving truck later, on a bittersweet day, with their children and grandchildren toting, arranging, and cheering them on, they were transported to a one-level ranch house across town.

A for-sale sign was never posted on their lawn. Like most transactions in a small town, word-of-mouth sufficed, and even before they'd moved, Lee and Mary Lee Comer's son, Ben, who'd grown up next door, had expressed an interest in the house. My father couldn't bear to sit through the negotiations, so I attended the parley at his request. Ben, my mother, and I sat at the kitchen table. No Realtors were present. Mom and Ben settled on an equitable amount in less than a minute, Mom threw in a riding lawnmower for the right to come back and sit on the front porch whenever they wished. Ben hugged Mom. Mom hugged Ben. Ben and I shook hands. Mom made us lunch. Done deal.

A few months later, Ben, his wife, Meg, and their two boys, Sam and Jake, settled in, and now sleep in those old bedrooms under the eaves and sled on the hill in the winter and play pitch-and-catch in the front yard in the summer. In the evening, when the sun is soft in the western sky and the heat has broken, they sit at the top of the hill behind the house and watch the deer come out to feed, and the boys roll down the hill and run back up and do it all over again.

I walk past every now and again, poking around the old haunts. The Quaker widows have passed on, but their descendants still populate the street, visiting back and forth, just like when I was a kid. I sometimes stand and watch the house and wish I had bought it and moved my family in, but my sons have rooted themselves in our house, just as I did on Broadway, and it wears well, like an old shirt fitting in all the right places. Though even now, thirty years after moving from that house, when I hear the word *home*, the house on Broadway still comes to mind.

In the past ten years, Phil has enjoyed speaking at conventions, colleges, libraries, and churches around the country. For a list of his upcoming appearances, or to schedule him for your event or organization, please visit www.PhilipGulley.org and click on the Events button.

Phil continues to pastor at Fairfield Friends Meeting near Indianapolis. You may download his weekly messages at www.PhilipGulley.org. Click on the GraceTalk button and enjoy! For directions to Fairfield Friends Meeting, visit www.FairfieldFriends.org.

To learn about Phil's other nonfiction, The Porch Talk series, visit www.philipgulleybooks.com.

To discover Phil's wonderful fictional world of Harmony, Indiana, visit www.harmonyseries.com.

Because of the volume of mail he receives, Phil is unable to respond to every written letter. But if you e-mail him at Phil@PhilipGulley.org, he'll respond in a timely manner.

Thank you.